Wrestling's Heroes and Villains

Wrestling's Heroes and Villains

An In-depth Look at
Wrestling's Cheats and Champions,
Masters and Miscreants

ROBERT PICARELLO

B●XTREE

First published 2001 by The Berkley Publishing Group, a division of Penguin Putnam Inc.,
New York, NY 10014

First published in Great Britain 2001 by Boxtree
an imprint of Pan Macmillan Ltd
Pan Macmillan, 20 New Wharf Road, London N1 9RR
Basingstoke and Oxford
Associated comapnies throughout the world
www.panmacmillan.com

ISBN 0 7522 2009 8

1 3 5 7 9 8 6 4 2

Printed by Mackays of Chatham PLC, Chatham, Kent

I'd like to dedicate this book to two men who have been heroes to me all my life—my two brothers, William and Charles Picarello.

Without their guidance, love, and inspiration, I very well may have turned out to be a real-life heel. They helped me to keep my nose clean and to the grindstone, and for that I am forever grateful. They not only are great brothers, they are, more important, special human beings.

Contents

Acknowledgments   xi

Introduction   xiii

MODERN-DAY HEELS AND HEROES   1

Tank Abbott   3

Kurt Angle   5

"Stone Cold" Steve Austin   9

Mike Awesome   13

Buff Bagwell   15

Chris Benoit   18

The Big Show   21

Big Vito   24

Bam Bam Bigelow   28

Steve Blackman   30

Booker T   32

Big Boss Man   35

D'Lo Brown   37

The Demon   39

Diamond Dallas Page   41

Disco Inferno   43

Shane Douglas   45

The Dudley Boyz   47

Edge & Christian   52

Faarooq   55

David Flair   57

Ric Flair   59

Mick Foley   62

Goldberg   67

Eddie Guerrero   72

The Hardy Boyz 74
Bret Hart 77
Hulk Hogan 81
Jeff Jarrett 85
Chris Jericho 89
Kane 93
Kidman 96
Konnan 98
Shane McMahon 100
Vince McMahon, Jr. 102
Kevin Nash 107
Rey Mysterio, Jr. 111
Right to Censor 114
Rikishi Phatu 116
Road Dogg 120
The Rock 122
Saturn 127
Scott Steiner 130
Al Snow 133
Sting 135
Lance Storm 139
Tazz 141
Too Cool 144
Triple H 146
The Undertaker 150
Vampiro 154
X-Pac 158

BEAUTIES AMONGST BEASTS **161**
Chyna 163
Debra 166
Major Gunns 168
Miss Hancock 170
Ivory 172
Jacqueline 174

The Kat 175

Lita 177

Stephanie McMahon 180

Terri Runnels 183

Trish Stratus 185

Tori 187

Torrie Wilson 189

LEGENDARY HEROES AND VILLAINS **191**

Andre the Giant 193

Terry Funk 196

"Superstar" Billy Graham 198

"Rowdy" Roddy Piper 200

Bruno Sammartino 202

George "The Animal" Steele 204

Acknowledgments

First on my list of thanks in helping make *Wrestling's Heroes and Villains* a reality is Tom Colgan and Kelly Sinanis. Without their dedication, help, and input, this book would have never gotten off the ground. Kelly, I must say I'm sorry that my Yankees beat your Mets in the World Series, but I am not sorry to have had the opportunity to work on another book with both you and Tom. Words cannot express my gratitude.

I would also again like to thank my family and friends for supporting me through another project. Know that even though we aren't always together, you are always on my mind and in my heart.

I would also like to personally welcome four new additions to our ever-growing family: Deanna Nicole Picarello, Danielle Marie Picarello, Gary Cassiliano, Jr., and Morgan Cassiliano. I wish each of you a life full of love, happiness, health, and prosperity.

Again I would like to thank Dov Teta, Robert Alvarez, and Tarah O'Brien for taking part and caring about what goes into these pages. I can't thank the three of you enough for your input and friendship.

Last, but not least, is the Silvestro family: Nicholas, Marie, Bart, Fay, Ariana, Nicole, Ralph and Mitch Caglioti, and the love of my life, Denise. Thank you all for being understanding during this project and thank you for accepting me into your home and family. Your kind words and actions never go unnoticed or unappreciated.

And, as always, a kiss above to my eyes in the sky; you too are always on my mind and in my heart.

Introduction

Pro wrestling is hotter than ever, and there have been many theories in the past couple of years as to why the once frowned-upon industry has turned into a multibillion-dollar business.

Some point to the exposure the grappling game has received from cable and free television,where the wrestling telecasts are routinely outdrawing major sports broadcasts such as Monday Night Football and the NBA playoffs. Others claim the twenty-four/seven information highway known as the Internet,where fans from all over the world can discuss their favorite topics whenever they so desire, is responsible. Still other pundits point to the admission by wrestling promoters that wrestling is sports-entertainment and not a true, competitive sport.

But the main reason for wrestling's popularity today is no different now than it was back in the olden days: the heels and the heroes. The champions and cheaters are the driving force behind the buzz.

Sure, there 's no doubt that the tremendous amount of mainstream exposure and modern-day technology have added to the popularity of the sports-entertainment business,but the bottom line for the fans tuning in and buying tickets is to see their favorite villains, vanquishers, and vixens in action.

Back in the 1970s, promoters would pack fans in to see typical good guys like Bruno Sammartino and Andre the Giant battle notorious bad guys like George "The Animal "Steele and "Superstar" Billy Graham. The 1980s were no different.All the little "Hulkamaniacs" would tune in to see Hulk Hogan and his clean-cut soldiers take on scoundrels like "Rowdy" Roddy Piper and his hooligans.

While the modern-day era is similar as wrestling is still good versus evil, the roles of the heels and heroes are somewhat different.The current heroes are no longer your milk-drinking, vitamin-eating,and say-your-prayers type of gladiators. The badder the hero today,the more pop he will receive from the wrestling audience.

For instance, "Stone Cold" Steve Austin may be one of wrestling's most popular heroes today, yet he is labeled as the meanest S.O.B. in the business. Goldberg is another beloved warrior, but his attitude and temperament leave him right on the verge of being out of control. The Rock, known as "The People's Champion," once even turned on the fans during his career — and the people still love him.

The heels are also more complex these days. No longer are they the ugly miscreants who come to the ring dressed in black, concealing foreign objects to use to their advantage during the match. Nowadays, these brutes not only openly display the weapons that they use in the ring,they also play the role of borderline psychopaths who should really be locked up instead of in the wrestling ring.

For instance,wrestling's top heel, Triple H, once kidnapped the boss's daughter and got "married" to Stephanie McMahon against her will in Las Vegas at a drive-through chapel while she was passed out in the seat next to him. This relentless radical has also made a name for himself on the grappling circuit by doing to other competitors what heels do best: kicking the living crap out of people.

Another modern-day badass in the biz is Jeff Jarrett,who not only has dubbed himself "The Chosen One" on the WCW circuit, but also likes to go around whacking people over the head with his trusty guitar.

Meanwhile, The Undertaker, who once battled his own brother, Kane, in an inferno match, where the idea was to set the other opponent on fire, has taken his new image and title in the WWF as "The American Badass" to heart. The dark warrior won't stop stomping on people until he has the world heavyweight title around his waist once again.

While the personalities of the good guys and bad guys may be somewhat different today as compared to yesteryear, the importance of each of their roles for one another remains the same. A baby face can only become a superstar if he has an equally super heel pitted against him night after night. The rivalries are what make the shows so popular and interesting. Throw in some beautiful babes like Chyna, Torrie Wilson, Lita, and Miss Hancock, and you have a recipe for success.

Just like in the movies,if the hero has no villains or obstacles thrown before him or her, where's the suspense and danger? Add some T&A to a well-thought-out script, and you have yourself a winner!

Wrestling's Heroes and Villains takes you on a journey with over fifty of today's modern-day babyfaces and heels. You will learn about their backgrounds and get the facts on each ring king and how they got to be either loved or hated on the grappling circuit.

Heroes and Villains also puts you in touch with some of the most luscious ladies on the mat scene. You will learn who likes to "show off" in the ring and who likes to give her opponent "head" whenever the opportunity calls for such action.

Inside, you will also venture back in time and get a look at the careers of some of wrestling's legendary heels and heroes. Read about squared-circle greats such as Bruno Sammartino, Terry Funk, Andre the Giant, and "Rowdy" Roddy Piper and how they paved the way for the modern-day stars.

So pull up your bootstraps and get ready to rumble.You may not believe who was once a heel and who was once a hero in their careers, but one thing is for certain, you'll enjoy the ride *Wrestling's Heroes and Villains* takes you on as it's chock-full of photos and info on all your favorite grappling greats . . . and not so greats!

Modern-Day Heroes and Villains

Tank Abbott

This wrestler, who is built like a Sherman tank, wasted no time becoming one of wrestling's most feared grapplers. The 6-foot, 265-pound brawler has the most feared right hand on the circuit. It doesn't matter who he's in the ring with, if he gets a chance to land his devastating punch, it's lights out for his foe!

In an *Inside Wrestling Digest* story, Mike Jones, formerly known as Virgil, claims that Abbott's lethal right is the most crushing blow in wrestling today.

"People have made fun of me because I've gotten whipped by the best in WCW," he said. "Yeah, I've felt the Stinger Splash, the Torture Rack, and the Spear more times than I can remember. Years ago, I was among the first to feel Yokozuna's Splash, but nothing, and I mean nothing, has knocked me as loopy as Tank Abbott's punch."

Abbott is a four-year veteran of the Ultimate Fighting Championship, where he fought in more fights (fourteen) than any other competitor and had the third most wins. In his debut UFC match against John Muta, he knocked out his opponent in an impressive twenty-one seconds. He made the successful transition from the UFC to the pro wrestling ranks with no problem, just like Ken Shamrock and Dan Severn before him.

"There's something about Tank's intensity that brings out the animal in a wrestler," Jones said.

When asked how he could make such an easy adjustment from the all-out, bloody wars of the UFC to the scripted plots of pro wrestling, he had this to say: "I've been wrestling since I was nine years old, and I've trained in boxing, but fighting isn't just boxing or wrestling. You just have to take from them what you can use in a fight."

The Huntington Beach, California, native was trained by former champion Bobby Eaton at the WCW Power Plant, and when he was ready to make his debut in the WCW, he shunned the idea of wrestling against the inexperienced journeymen. Instead, the bald, goateed fighter grabbed a front-row seat at a Nitro broadcast and challenged Rick Steiner, who is considered to be one of the toughest pros out there, to a match.

One of his biggest matches ever came at a WCW SuperBrawl, where he took on one of his own, Big Al, also a former UFC competitor. The match was a good-old-fashioned barroom brawl, where the object was to retrieve a leather jacket hanging on a pole. But as soon as the bell rang, the jacket became secondary as Abbott and Al went full-throttle at each other.

Most of the match had Big Al taking it to the Tank, but as is always the case with Abbott, he only needs that one moment, that one split second to land the hand, which he did, and it was all over but the crying!

Kurt Angle

At first glance, you can be thrown off as to whether or not Kurt Angle is a heel or hero—his clean-cut boyish good looks can be deceiving. As a matter of fact, this guy would throw his mother off the mat if it meant his becoming the world wrestling champion! But anyway, when Angle first came onto the 'rassling scene, he was introduced as this all-American athlete who had represented his country at the Olympics and won a gold medal in—what else—wrestling and was all about goodness and "the truth." The 6-foot-2, 220-pound grappler

Howard Kemats

even enters the ring decked out in America's red, white, and blue, wearing his Olympic gold medal around his neck—the epitome of all that is wholesome and American. But as soon as he opens his mouth, it's all over. Anything but the truth seems to pass from his lips. He tries to make everyone believe that he is all righteous, when in fact he is just the opposite. A perfect example of this is his so-called concern for his "friend" Stephanie McMahon-Helmsley. When Stephanie was having "marital" problems with her husband, Hunter Hearst Helmsley, he offered to be her shoulder to cry on. He even told her one night: "If you need anything at all Stephanie, I'll always be there as a friend."

Well, the writing was on the wall. For a man who claims to be all about intelligence, integrity, and intensity, he was starting to show his true colors more often, and they definitely weren't red, white, and blue. As a matter of fact, they seem to be more on the yella side. Angle definitely wanted to be more than just friends with Mrs. Helmsley, and he was prepared to do whatever he had to in order to win her love. Sometimes the Pittsburgh, Pennsylvania, native seems to be more about stupidity, deceit, and weakness. Angle has been getting into situations like this ever since he broke onto the scene, and he gets there mostly on his lying and seems to only get what he wants by striking when a person is most vulnerable. When asked about his relationship with Stephanie, Angle wanted to know "where is it written that a guy and girl can't be just friends?"

In August 2000 at SummerSlam, Angle was scheduled to be involved in a Triple-Threat match for the World Heavyweight championship with The Rock and Triple H. A couple of days prior to this match on SmackDown!, the Angle and Triple H situation came to a head when Hunter found out that Angle had planted a big wet one on Stephanie's lips while she lay helpless, dazed, and confused backstage on a couch after taking a blow in the ring. Triple H was not around at the time because he was in the ring taking a pounding for Angle, whom he had rushed out to help during one of his matches.

When Triple H confronted his wife at SummerSlam about the lip-locking that had gone on between her and Angle, Stephanie placed the blame directly on Angle. She claimed that it was all a blur to her and that she had no feelings for Angle. "Kurt took advantage of me," she explained. "He kissed me, and I had no idea as to what was going on."

Upon making his entrance during SummerSlam, Angle took hold of the mic and tried to clear up what had happened between him and the very-married Stephanie:

"A lot of people are expecting an apology from me for kissing Stephanie on SmackDown!" Angle said on that summer night. "Well, the fact of the matter is, I would like to apologize. I would like to apologize for not doing it a heck of a lot sooner. I am an Olympic gold medalist. See these medals. I didn't get these for backing down or second-guessing myself. I'll leave that up to you people. I did what I had to do, and I am damn proud of it. I am what you people call a given. I give my all in this ring—I gave my all in honoring my country in the Olympic games, and Triple H, I gave your wife what you could never give her even if your life depended on it. And that's *the truth*!"

The real truth about this young wrestler is that, although he may be a weasel, he is a surefire winner with the crowd. His deceit generates heat not only with the wrestling crowds and viewers, but also with his in-ring opponents.

Angle is a rarity in pro wrestling today as he was able to make the transition from amateur wrestling to pro wrestling without any wrinkles in his game. He has taken the WWF by storm and there's no limit to what this former gold medalist can achieve in the ring.

Having only made his pro debut in December of 1999, it's amazing how fast he's climbed the ladder of success in the WWF. He has already worn the Intercontinental and European championship belts and was even crowned 2000 King of the Ring in June. Then on October 22, 2000, Kurt Angle won wrestling's most-coveted belt, the World Heavyweight title. Angle won the strap from "The People's Champion," The Rock, at a No Mercy event in Albany, New York.

The all-around athlete not only won a gold medal at the 1996 Olympic Games in Atlanta in the 220-pound freestyle wrestling competition, he also had a tryout with the National Football League's Pittsburgh Steelers in 1995, even though he had not played college ball. The chiseled wrestler can also max bench press 420 pounds and even squat 630 pounds without a problem.

Before he became a pro wrestler, Angle had even tried his hand, or mouth in this case, at sportscasting. He worked as a sportscaster for Fox Sports for a year, but found out commenting about sports wasn't his "angle." He wanted to be right in the middle of the action instead of reporting about it. That's when he turned to the WWF and Vince McMahon, who had previously contacted Kurt right after his Olympic victory about joining the organization, but Angle had declined at the time.

Angle had never even watched a WWF event until the summer of

1998, and when he liked what he saw, he called the federation's head honcho and asked him if the offer still stood for him to join in on the fun. McMahon agreed to give the kid from Pennsylvania a try, and he has been golden ever since to say the least.

Whether or not he's a heel or hero is for the viewer to decide, but one thing that's for certain is Kurt knows what Angle's to take in order to make it to the top!

"Stone Cold" Steve Austin

How can anyone so bad be so good? "Stone Cold" Steve Austin has the reputation of being the meanest S.O.B. in the business today, but the fans adore him anyway.

Pics Pix

One of the main reasons he is so loved throughout the country is that Steve Austin does what he wants, when he wants, and, more impressively, to whomever he wants! Call him what you want. Call him a rebel. I'll agree. Call him a loner. I'm right there with you. Call him tough. I've got your back. Call him defiant. I'll second that notion.

But the best word to use when it comes down to describing this hero of the ring is plain and simple: winner. He has fought his way to the top of the wrestling mountain after many years of blood, sweat, and beers—not tears. "Stone Cold" doesn't know the meaning of the word *cry*. Then again, he's made many a grown man cry on several occasions.

Ever since his King of the Ring victory on June 23, 1996, over Jake "The Snake" Roberts, the world of sports-entertainment has never been the same. This was also the infamous night when the Austin 3:16 moniker was born.

Austin read Roberts the riot act after he beat him for the King title and, as he recalls, he ad-libbed the whole thing. "So, after I beat Jake, he was walking up the aisle [and] basically what I said to a T was, 'You sit there and you thump your Bible and say your prayers, and it didn't get you anywhere. You talk about your psalms. You talk about John 3:16. Well, Austin 3:16 said I just whipped your ass!' It was completely ad-libbed."

Whether it was ad-libbed or scripted doesn't matter. It stuck and stuck royally. Austin 3:16 signs, shirts, bumper stickers, buttons, posters—you name it—were being sold! He was not only becoming a wrestling hero, but also a marketing champion. All because of a statement he made after a grappling victory.

No one could have predicted that this former dockworker/college football star would have made such a tremendous impact on the wrestling industry. His success is mind-boggling because he doesn't have a gimmick, and he isn't the biggest wrestler in the WWF either. While he is 6 foot 2 and weighs in at 252 pounds, those numbers can't even compare to such monsters as The Undertaker, who's 6 foot 10, 328 pounds, or his scary looking brother, Kane, who's 7 foot, 326 pounds. Hell, you want huge? How 'bout The Big Show, who rumbles in at 7 foot 2, 500 pounds?

You would think that Austin wouldn't stand a chance against these mammoths, but as the saying goes, you can't judge a book by its cover. As a matter of fact, Austin is a man who doesn't live by anyone's book or rules, and his boss and WWF owner, Vince McMahon, found that out the hard way!

McMahon should have known that once the bald badass set foot into his federation Austin wouldn't be pushed around. His comments from when he first signed on with the WWF should have made that perfectly clear:

"I'll tell ya what, McMahon and the rest better not try to put me in many tags or try to kiss up to me like we're friends or something.

I'll go right up to that office and open up a whole six-pack of whoop ass."

And in the days and years that followed, he held true to those words. Many an opponent fell victim to his lethal "Stone Cold" Stunner, including McMahon. And you can bet your ass that there are many more victims to come.

Though "Stone Cold" is a man of few words, his fans hang on to whatever he utters as gospel, and he likes to do his talking in the ring. He also likes to take matters into his own hands. He lives by the DTA motto of "Don't Trust Anyone," and so far in his career, he has stuck to his guns.

One particular incident that he took into his own hands came about in November 1999 at the Survivor Series when he was mowed down by the speeding car of an unknown driver. The accident not only nearly cost him his livelihood, but also his life. He vowed to get revenge on the coward behind the wheel. The driver knew that he or she couldn't beat him on the mat, so he or she took an unsuspecting Austin out with a car on that unfortunate night.

The plot was played out in "who shot JR?" fashion with the WWF listing the suspects upon Austin's return in September 2000. But the Texas Rattlesnake took this as neither joke nor plot, he took it "Stone Cold" serious. He vowed to find this person and give them the biggest ass whooping of his or her life. Was it his best friend, Jim Ross? Was it Stephanie McMahon-Helmsley, the wife of Triple H, whom Austin was chasing the night he got hit? Was it The Rock, who has never defeated SCSA and who also once threw Austin off a bridge? Was it The Big Show, who got his chance at winning the WWF world title belt that night only because Austin wasn't there to participate? Or was it the federation owner, Vince McMahon, who was trying to rid himself of a problem-child employee?

The case in point here was that it didn't matter who it was. Whether it was his arch rival or best friend, it didn't matter. Austin was on a mission, and he was bound to get the sorry ass, no matter what it took for SCSA to get even. He was prepared to fight the odds and whoever else got in his way.

This is the way it's been ever since Austin got into the wrestling business. He has made a lucrative living out of never leaving any unfinished business.

So far in his illustrious career, "Stone Cold" has compiled four WWF world heavyweight titles, two Intercontinental belts, and three WWF tag straps. He also holds the Royal Rumble title from 1998 and the King of the Ring title from 1996. Earlier in his wrestling career, he won titles in the WCW that included the TV, tag and U.S. belts.

Austin won his first WWF world title against "The Heartbreak Kid" Shawn Michaels on March 29, 1998, in Boston, Massachusetts, at WrestleMania XIV, and from then on he became a marked man. McMahon threw everyone imaginable in Austin's way to try to knock him off his perch, but usually Austin found a way to get the W. Even the ones who beat him usually didn't have very long to celebrate.

Take Kane, for instance. The Big Red Machine managed to beat "Stone Cold" one night (June 28, 1998) at a First Blood Match in a King of the Ring event held in Pittsburgh, Pennsylvania, thus becoming the new WWF champ. But the taste of victory didn't last very long as Austin defeated the mask-wearing wrestler the very next night in Cleveland, Ohio.

The bottom line here is, as long as Steve Austin is healthy, no one— good or evil—will ever get in his way. So they should all stay the "Hell, Yeah!" out of his way because "Stone Cold" says so!

Mike Awesome

Here is a wrestler who truly lives up to his name. Mike Awesome was lured over to World Championship Wrestling from Extreme Championship Wrestling (ECW) by Vince Russo and Eric Bischoff. The two head honchos want Awesome to be one of the new main eventers that will take over for the older talent that used to make up the federation.

Awesome not only is blessed with raw power and ring charisma, but also likes to take on opponents with a gritty, hard-core style. The 6-foot-6, 292-pound heavyweight has the graceful moves of a lesser weight class, but don't let that fool you, this grappler can pummel anyone who steps through the ropes.

It's no wonder he grew up to become a professional wrestler as he was born in Tampa, Florida, a hotbed for pro grappling talent. Tampa also raised and groomed wrestling superstars such as Hulk Hogan, Randy "Macho Man" Savage, Dusty Rhodes, and "Mr. Wonderful" Paul Orndoff.

As a matter of fact, Awesome squared off against his neighbor Hulk Hogan one night in Birmingham, Alabama, and gave the Hulkster a hometown ass kicking. The match was a main event in the Jefferson Civic Center, and it was a classic battle of rookie versus veteran.

Hogan tried everything in his power and reach to take out Awesome, but on this night the youngster was simply too awesome. Hogan even hit him with foreign objects such as chairs—including decking him with a weightlifting belt—but it had no effect on the former ECW star.

Awesome got the win on this night, which was tainted by Billy Kidman interfering in the match and landing a chair blow on Hogan. In reality the interference only saved Hogan from getting more of a beating from Awesome.

"I felt sorry for him in there," Awesome said after the match. "Hogan's trying to stand in there with the most lethal force in wrestling and doesn't even realize he's risking his life. You know, it could have been a lot worse if I hadn't felt sorry for him."

The up-and-comer trained in his home state under the watchful eye of Steve Keirn, and then was discovered by a Japanese wrestling scout during one of his tune-up matches. He went to Japan and fought overseas for eight years in the country's FMW promotion under the ring name of The Gladiator.

When he came back to the States he hooked up with ECW, where he eventually garnered the world championship title. As a matter of fact, when Awesome made his debut with WCW on April 10, 2000, it was under controversial circumstances as he was still the ECW champ at the time.

He came onto the scene in awesome fashion as Mike attacked an ailing Kevin Nash while he was delivering a WCW promo on a Nitro broadcast. The surprise attacker went to work on the injured Nash before a stunned crowd as he beat the WCW mega star with Nash's own crutches. It was clearly a memorable entrance.

But while this wrestler may be awesome in the ring, the fact of the matter still remains that he bolted ECW, a federation who stood by him through his growing pains and made him what he is today, without hesitation. If he turned his back that quickly on people like ECW owner Paul Heyman, who's to say that he won't do it again to the fans or the powers-that-be in the WCW.

You need look no further than Awesome's comment to writer Dave Lenker of *Wrestling Digest*: "I'm willing to do whatever it takes to be on top. I'll stop at nothing."

Buff Bagwell

Although Buff Bagwell is bet-ter known for his successes as a tag-teamer, he definitely has the stuff to make it on the singles cir-cuit. The tough-as-nails grappler made his pro debut more than ten years ago and was immediately a hit with both the male and female fans. The men wanted to have his physique, while the women lusted over his chiseled body.

Howard Kernats

The Georgia native began his career in 1990, wrestling under the name of Fabian for All Star Wrestling, located in his home state. While at All Star, he was paired with Chris Walker, and it took the two no time to capture the federation's tag team belts. A year later, he had not only changed his ring name, but also federation's. Bagwell moved on to Global Wrestling, where he was known as "the Handsome Stranger."

His time in the spotlight at Global got him noticed and in 1992, World Championship Wrestling came calling. Immediately they changed his name to Marcus Bagwell and put him on the tag circuit, where he was paired with 2 Cold Scorpio. The twosome hit it off in the ring and immediately became fan favorites. Before you knew it, they were going for the gold. On October 4, 1993, in Columbus, Georgia, Bagwell and Scorpio faced the Nasty Boys for the WCW tag title, and

Marcus wouldn't disappoint his hometown fans as he and 2 Cold came away with the victory and belts that night.

Less than a month later at Halloween Havoc in New Orleans, the duo would lose the straps to the same Nasty Boys, but Bagwell didn't care as he was now in the big time and on his way to not only becoming a star in the federation, but more important, being voted WCW Rookie of the Year. When his tag partner eventually left the federation, Bagwell hooked up with The Patriot and formed a new pairing called Stars and Stripes.

Together, Bagwell and The Patriot would win the tag championship twice. And they earned their stripes by making their opponents see stars. They won their first title on September 25, 1994, against a team known as Pretty Wonderful. The Wonderful duo got their revenge on October 23 at Halloween Havoc in Detroit, Michigan, when they won the belts back from the Stars and Stripes tandem.

But the S&S team would have a pretty wonderful laugh in the end as Bagwell and The Patriot again beat their foes for the belts on November 16 at the Clash of the Champions XXIX in sunny Jacksonville, Florida. Twenty-two days later, they lost their titles to the Harlem Heat in Atlanta, Georgia.

In 1995, Bagwell again took on another teammate and led him to golden tag pastures. The 6-foot-1, 247-pound tag specialist was now sharing the spotlight with Scotty Riggs as the American Males tag team. The two struck gold on September 18, 1995, at the Fall Brawl in Johnson City, Tennessee, where they defeated the Harlem Heat for the straps. But the duo held on to the belts for only eleven days because the Harlem Heat won them back in Bagwell's home state on September 27 in Atlanta, Georgia.

In 1996, Bagwell wanted to try something different. Hulk Hogan was calling any and all WCWers to latch on to his defiant group, the New World Order, that was looking to take over the federation. Bagwell decided to turn in his babyface and go heel. He abandoned Riggs and the American Males and went for the black and white of the nWo. He no longer wanted that clean-cut, loverboy image. Instead he wanted to be on the dark side. As a matter of fact, Buff, as he was now known, was paired with Scott Norton for a while and they were known around the ranks as the "Vicious & Delicious" pair. He also teamed with "Big Poppa Pump" Scott Steiner for a while and the twosome ran roughshod over the WCW for some time.

Just when it looked like his career was going to take off, he suffered a major setback that not only almost cost him his wrestling career, but also the feeling in his body. On April 22, 1998, on a nationally televised match against Rick Steiner, Bagwell severely injured his spinal cord and neck in front of millions of viewers and fans.

Buff not only showed that he had the stuff to return, but he also proved he could still be a force in the ring. Ten months after his scare in the ring he was back pummeling opponents. He would even strike gold again not too long after the accident when he won the tag title with "The Franchise" Shane Douglas on April 4, 2000.

The wrestler who combines a unique blend of power and quickness has proven over his career that he has what it takes to be a major player in the wrestling world. The only thing left for this wrestling superstar is to decide where he wants to strut his stuff—on the good side or the dark side.

Chris Benoît

Howard Kernats

Pound-for-pound, Chris Benoit can certainly be considered the strongest wrestler in the game today. He is also by far one of best technical and underrated grapplers to ever come onto the pro wrestling scene. Standing at a mere 5 foot 10, and weighing 220 pounds, the native of Canada seems to be at a disadvantage whenever he steps between the ropes, but once the bell sounds everyone in attendance witnesses his unbelievable mat skills.

Benoit was born in Montreal, where he lived for the first twelve years of his life until his family moved four provinces west to Edmonton, Alberta. He took in his first pro match at the Northlands Agricon, a Stampede Wrestling event, where he saw the man he would soon work to emulate in every possible way: Tom Billington, a.k.a. The Dynamite Kid.

The young wrestler took notice of everything his idol did and tried to incorporate it into his repertoire. To this day, like the Dynamite Kid, he is supremely conditioned, having muscles on top of his muscles, and utilizes impressive, high-flying moves as part of his lethal arsenal.

"Ever since I first laid my eyes on the Dynamite Kid I've tried to emulate him," Benoit said. "I've tried to look like him, walk like him, and talk like him. I'd spend time in my bedroom throwing punches and kicks at the bed pretending to be him. I started lifting weights at thirteen to try and clone myself after him. He definitely lit a fire inside me that still burns strong today, and that is the passion I have for professional wrestling."

Benoit has found success wherever he has gone, on foreign soil such as Mexico and Japan, in Philadelphia's Extreme Championship Wrestling (where he got the nickname Canadian Crippler for breaking the neck of an opponent in the ring), and in the WCW, where he had the honor of wearing several championship belts, including the world heavyweight title, which he abandoned hours after he won it to start a new chapter in his wrestling career in the WWF.

On January 31, 2000, Chris Benoit made his WWF debut as he, along with Dean Malenko, Perry Saturn, and Eddie Guerrero took seats at ringside, only to later become involved with the New Age Outlaws. This was the start of something big for the wrestler who is comparatively small in stature to his foes.

In less than four months, April 2, 2000, in his WrestleMania debut, he captured his first WWF title as he took control of the Intercontinental Championship from Kurt Angle. One month later, May 8, 2000, after losing the Intercontinental Championship to Chris Jericho four days earlier on a SmackDown! telecast, Benoit recaptured the IC title belt on Monday Night Raw. These action-packed confrontations were also building up a huge rivalry between the two young guns.

Benoit was meanwhile becoming a ruthless warrior in the ring, where no one was safe. Everything he did between the ropes had a purpose, and he began to show more intensity and determination than ever before in his career. He was also developing quite the mean streak.

One person who felt his wrath, believe it or not, was Chyna. As I said, no one was safe, and she found out the hard way what it was to be in the wrong place at the wrong time one night in July 2000. This was to be the night that Benoit solidified himself as a heel in the federation.

On July, 3, 2000, in Orlando, Florida, Benoit took part in a bout with Eddie Guerrero and won by disqualification because Chyna had interfered in the match. When it was over, Guerrero tried to get Benoit back but misfired with a dropkick that laid out Chyna. The Canadian

Crippler then blasted Guerrero with his own European belt as Eddie was checking on his "Mamacita."

The best—or worst—was yet to come as Benoit applied his Crippler Crossface on Chyna for a long while before the officials could finally break it up. On that night, announcer Jim Ross put Benoit over as a "mega-heel," claiming that he doesn't give a damn who he hurts.

Ross was correct as, later in the night, the new badass struck again. He came onto the scene as the main event match between Shane Mc-Mahon and The Rock was about to begin. Before the two had even gotten started, Benoit came out and nailed The Rock from behind with a chair. He locked the Crippler Crossface on "The People's Champion" as the young McMahon kicked The Rock in the midsection. WWF officials had a difficult time breaking this mess up, but the hold was finally broken by Mick Foley. When all was said and done Benoit's only reaction was to smile sadistically.

With the son of the boss now by his side, there was no telling how far Benoit would go. As a matter of fact, the lethal wrestler almost made it to the top of the WWF mountain with Shane at his side. On July 23, 2000, at a Fully Loaded event in Dallas, Texas, Benoit touched WWF heavy-weight gold for a brief second in a main event match against The Rock.

In a crazy match where Shane interfered something awful with chairs and cheapshots, Benoit was granted the win as a result of a DQ (disqualification) granted by the ref. And just when everyone thought there was a new WWF world champ in Benoit, out walks Commissioner Mick Foley, who overturns the ref's decision and orders the match to continue, citing that there was no disqualification. The Rock then proceeded to defend his title and remain champ.

Even though he didn't walk out of the arena that night with the heavyweight strap, it seems certain that Benoit is destined for the top slot sometime in the near future, but until then, he'll just keep "crippling" his opponents!

The Big Show

Paul Wight, a.k.a. The Big Show and The Giant, has made a huge impact on the wrestling world both as a baby face and as a heel. He learned the tricks of the trade at WCW's training grounds, the Power Plant, and then made an impressive entrance in the industry in 1995, when he burst on the WCW scene as The Giant, claiming to be legendary Andre the Giant's long-lost son.

The rookie grappler tried to play hero right off the bat as he pretended to only want to defend his "in-his-dreams" father's honor. He didn't toil around with mid-card personalities upon entering the federation. Instead, he went right after the top dog, Hulk Hogan, citing that the Hulkster was responsible for many of the wrongs in his late, great dad's life.

This association immediately put the new kid, well, giant in his case, on the block in the limelight. In his first few months on the pro scene, The Giant went out of his way to make Hogan's life miserable. He enjoyed in a big way wreaking havoc on the wrestling legend's life. On October 29, 1995, at Halloween Havoc in Detroit, the two squared off in a Monster Truck match and, by the end of the event, The Giant sat atop the WCW mountain as the new world champion.

This would be only the beginning of his successes in the WCW. He would go on to win one more world title (over Ric Flair on April 22, 1996, in Albany, Georgia) and three tag-team belts in his career with the organization. Amazingly, the big guy would garner the tag straps with three different partners (Lex Luger, Sting, and Scott Hall) during his time on the tag circuit. He had many alliances in his time with the WCW, and he often went back and forth from hero to heel. One such circumstance was in 1998, during his reign as tag champ with Sting.

Sting was a clean-cut-to-the-bone wrestler and wanted no part of dirty-wrestling factions such as the nWo, and when The Giant turned heel and joined the posse, Sting spat in his teammate's face to show his disapproval. This was the beginning of the end of their tag team and the start of a feud between the two grapplers. Their score was settled later that year at the Great American Bash event, where The Giant defeated his former ally in less than seven minutes.

Wight would make the big jump to the WWF in February 1999, when again he made a huge entrance. He literally burst onto the scene as he ripped through the ring canvas at the St. Valentine's Day Massacre and grabbed a hold of "Stone Cold" Steve Austin and threw him through a steel cage.

Howard Kernats

He immediately aligned himself with the federation boss, Vince Mc-Mahon, as part of Team Corporate, and he again tried to play hero as the last line of defense for the WWF head honcho. But, as has been the case throughout his whole career, Wight jumped ship and rebelled against Team Corporate and McMahon. The mountain-of-a-wrestler felt he was taking too much abuse from Vince and The Rock of Team Corporate. As a matter of fact, the situation came to a head at WrestleMania XV when Wight knocked out his boss after McMahon slapped him in the face following The Big Show's match against ManKind. His own words, which were really meant for ManKind before their bout that night were: "Now you've woken a sleeping giant!" That statement really was a warning to McMahon and the rest of the WWF.

In the months that followed, he tore up the scene, knocking down any and all in his path. He teamed with another giant, The Undertaker, in August 1999 in Minneapolis, Minnesota, to win the tag title. The awesome duo would then take part in some action-packed matches with The Rock and Mankind, as the pairings traded tag titles three times over the course of their meetings.

But the best was yet to come. By November 1999, the 7-foot-2, 500-pound wrestler was wearing the heavyweight title strap around his waist courtesy of his defeating Triple H at the Survivor Series held in Detroit. This was quite a feat considering the Tampa native had only been in the federation for a mere nine months. Some wrestlers go a whole lifetime waiting for a chance to just take part in a world title match, let alone win one!

The Big Show wound up putting on a funny show when he appeared as a guest on *Saturday Night Live* last year and decided to try yet another image change in the ring. This change wasn't a stretch for the muscular giant, as he was bringing his true life persona, which includes making people laugh, to the mat.

Since the change, some of the characters Wight has appeared as were The Big Showbowski and the Fat Bastard character from the Austin Powers movie. No one knows what's next for this WWF superstar, but one thing is for certain, and that's "The Show" will go on!

Big Vito

One thing is for certain, Vito LoGrasso, a.k.a. Big Vito, is no ma-maluke. This Brooklyn native is a bad-to-the-bone type of wrestler who can battle with the best of 'em.

LoGrasso grew up in the predominantly Italian neighborhood of Bensonhurst, Brooklyn, where the tough got tougher and the weak moved to Queens. He picked up some tricks of his eventual wrestling trade from the mean streets as he had to fend for himself on more than one occasion. LoGrasso found out the hard way that growing up in Brooklyn was about more than playing stickball and drinking egg creams: It was survival.

In the winter of 1990, while watching a wrestling show on the tube, the then–freight company worker believed that he could make a living in the ring, so he decided to sign up at the Johnny Rodz School of Wrestling, located in Gleason's Gym in downtown Brooklyn.

He would train there three nights a week for the next six months with grapplers such as Tazz, Tommy Dreamer, and High Morrus, who not only taught him the ins and outs of the business, but also taught him how to take a beating. The veterans were pretty rough on the local kid, but in the end, it paid off for him as he not only gained their respect, but also was on his way to wrestling stardom.

LoGrasso worked the local and independent circuits for quite some time before he was approached by Kendo Nagasaki of the NOW Wrestling Federation to grapple overseas in Japan. NOW was a small federation, but the young gun didn't care, he just wanted a chance to prove himself. After getting his feet wet in the Orient, he returned to the States in 1991 and held a position as a jobber for the World Wrestling Federation, where he worked with WWF superstars Bret Hart, The Undertaker and others. Not bad for someone who had only been in the mat game for less than a year.

While the federation liked his work, they never found a place for him full-time. He then moved on to the United States Wrestling Association in Tennessee for a little while and eventually plied his trade for three years in Puerto Rico under Carlos Colon of the World Wrestling Council.

When the wrestler, who first broke into the wrestling world as Skull Von Krush, finished up in the WWC, he returned home to an offer he couldn't refuse. Shohei "Giant" Baba heard about the up-and-coming wrestler and wanted LoGrasso to work with him in the All-Japan promotion. While this would again mean traveling overseas, Vito didn't care as All-Japan was the big time!

In his very first match LoGrasso made a name for himself, but it wasn't on purpose. He achieved something in the promotion that no one had done in five years—pinning the great Mitsuhara Misawa.

"I was in a battle royal," he said in an interview with *WCW Magazine*, "but you had to be pinned to be eliminated." He said to himself: "I have to pin someone before I'm eliminated." He found himself standing in the ring looking at the other wrestler. "He had green tights on and looked stupid, so I figured I could pin him. Baba pushed him forward, I attacked him like a cat, gave him a stunner and pinned him. The place went nuts. When I went to the back, someone informed me I pinned someone who hadn't been pinned in five years."

Now beaming with confidence, he returned to the States expecting to have offers waiting for him, but it wasn't to be. LoGrasso then proceeded to meet up with one of his training buddies, Tazz, from Gleason's Gym, and asked for some help obtaining work at Extreme Championship Wrestling, where Tazz was employed.

LoGrasso made the most of this opportunity, working his way up the ECW ladder in no time. In November 1999, he got the call he had been waiting for—Vince Russo, one of LoGrasso's longtime friends, from World Championship Wrestling had a spot for him if he wanted it.

He would be paired with an up-and-comer, Johnny the Bull, to form an all-Italian duo known as The Mamalukes. The Mamalukes were first brought on to shake down Disco Inferno for some cash that he owed to a very well-known Italian family in, where else, Brooklyn. When Inferno refused the offer he wasn't suppose to refuse, The Mamalukes, in typical hitmen fashion, worked him over along with a couple of his friends. These actions put them over with the fans, and in no time, the two thugs were wearing the tag straps.

On January 19, 1999, during a Thunder broadcast, The Mamalukes knocked off David Flair and Crowbar in Evansville, Indiana, for the right to be called tag-team champions. This was the first gold of LoGrasso's career, and he didn't stop there. He moved on to the singles circuit and garnered the Hardcore title. But, while the title meant more respectability for the Italian stallion, it also had a price.

Howard Kernats

In typical heel fashion, Big Vito turned on two of his colleagues who had helped him pave his way in the WCW, Vince Russo and Johnny the Bull. The big guy knew from his upbringing in a tough Brooklyn neighborhood that it's kill or be killed, and he definitely wanted to end up on the winning end.

Big Vito defeated wrestling legend Terry Funk on June 12, 2000, for the Hardcore Title in Richmond, Virginia, and the wrestler with an attitude finally got his just due. Where this hard-core wrestler, who now resides on Staten Island, takes his career is totally up to him. In the meantime, the other grapplers in the federation shouldn't fuggedabout Big Vito because they may very well find out the true meaning of being whacked. Or worse yet, they may find themselves swimming with the fishes.

Bam Bam Bigelow

Howard Kernats

Here's a guy you wouldn't want to run into in a dark alley. Bam Bam Bigelow not only stands at 6 foot 3, and weighs 325 pounds, he also has flames tattooed on the side of his head. Anyone crazy enough to step into the ring with a man who paid to have a needle carve a permanent image on his cranium has to be even crazier than Bigelow is.

The intimidating grappler trained in the mid-eighties at the famous Monster Factory with Larry Sharpe. The two would work together again in the World Class territory, after Bigelow moved on from the factory and teamed up to win the federation's version of the TV title. Bigelow would then ply his trade on the independent circuits before taking his game overseas.

The giant-sized wrestler tore up the scene on both the Japanese and German circuits and, for his efforts, was deemed "The Beast from the East." He was known for not only beating his opponents in the ring for the win, but also for terrorizing them out of their trunks. No one was safe in Bigelow's presence.

The Beast even left the legends cowering in fear. Upon arriving in the Orient in 1987, he stormed the New Japan wrestling organization and challenged their top grappler, the renowned Antonio Inoki. He also has been known to crash the Big Two, the World Wrestling Federation and World Championship Wrestling, here in the States on occasion.

He made a big splash in the WWF in April 1995, when he squared off against NFL Hall-of-Fame linebacker Lawrence Taylor at WrestleMania, but was released soon afterward and rumored to be "too difficult to manage" and "out of control."

Speaking of being out of control, he once burst onto the WCW scene in late 1998 demanding a match with one of their top dogs, Goldberg. When he realized that his words were getting him nowhere, he put his words into action and began "attacking" Goldberg. In 1999, he teamed with a few guys, Diamond Dallas Page and Kanyon, who were just as sadistic as him. Calling themselves The Triad, they racked up a couple of tag titles along the way with DDP and Bigelow winning one on May 31, 1999, in Houston, Texas, and DDP and Kanyon winning another on June 13, 1999, in Baltimore.

When that trio ran its course, Bigelow teamed with some other old colleagues, Chris Candido and Shane Douglas. Together they wreaked havoc on the federation as Triple Threat. Bam Bam would also go on his own and defeat Brian Knobs for the Hardcore title on February 7, 2000, in Tulsa, Oklahoma.

Whether alone or with partners, Bigelow has proven that he is a mean fighting machine who has tremendous ability for someone his size. The Beast is all about being bad, and when it comes to wrestling, he's hard-core through and through.

Steve Blackman

Howard Kernats

Steve Blackman didn't get the nickname Lethal Weapon for nothing. He is not only a threat to win every time he steps into the ring, he is also a threat to his opponents' health each time he enters an arena.

Blackman's arsenal is filled with menacing wrestling maneuvers such as his signature—The Guillotine—and he also possesses martial arts skills, which makes him doubly dangerous to his foes. The Annville, Pennsylvania, native impresses crowds with his lightning-quick kicks and punches, and usually leaves his opponents, no matter their size, shape, or status, begging for the bell.

At SummerSlam 2000, he faced Shane McMahon, the son of the federation's owner, Vince McMahon, and showed no mercy. Shane took on the dangerous grappler and lost badly. The two battled way above the ring on a ladder and Blackman knocked his opponent to the ground and then proceeded to leap on McMahon to get the pin and the win.

This victory allowed Blackman to regain the Hardcore belt he had previously lost to the owner's son on a Raw telecast six days prior to the summer event. Before losing the belt to McMahon, Blackman had won the Hardcore title on June 29, 2000, from Crash Holly on a SmackDown! broadcast.

The 6-foot-2, 246-pounder got his start on the wrestling circuit in Puerto Rico, and then went over to Japan and Canada to wrestle before making his way back to the United States. When Blackman finally got the call from the WWF, his stint was cut short because he'd contracted malaria on a South African tour and needed time off to recover.

When he returned to the action, he formed a partnership with another no-holds-barred specialist, Ken Shamrock, and together they made their ring competitors quiver. Blackman also got involved in the singles circuit and had an ongoing feud with Jeff Jarrett, before Double J left for the WCW.

While Blackman has been criticized for not having a true ring personality, the belief here is that he doesn't need one, as long as he has the skills to keep piling up the Ws. His character has taken on more of an edge lately, which has made his popularity skyrocket, but gimmicks and character traits don't make him a winner, his own, natural, "lethal weapons" do.

Booker T

Howard Kernats

To question whether or not Booker T is a good guy or a bad guy is like asking what color the American flag is—red, white, or blue?

The Texas native is all about good. The 6-foot-3, 250-pound grappler is good in the ring, good to his fans, and good-looking. Hell, Booker even looks good outside the arena in his designer threads! But don't get fooled by his *GQ* looks out of the squared circle, because once this chiseled athlete steps onto the mat, he's all about making his opponent look bad.

He's blessed with a body that's ripped and pumped beyond belief, and with an arsenal of wrestling maneuvers that's second to none; it's no wonder he has won over fifteen titles in his illustrious career. This graceful grappler usually picks apart his opponents in stunning fashion before he finishes them off with one of his signature maneuvers: a missile dropkick or an axe kick.

In June 2000, Booker, who had made his pro debut in 1989, really showed his good side as he took on the role of G.I. Bro, a great American hero. This character was very attractive to him at the time. He felt it was a role he could play in which he was still able to kick some serious butt in the ring while also maintaining his position as a role model for the children who were watching.

In an interview conducted by Jason Shaya for WCW.com, Booker said, "G. I. Bro is another aspect of the show. It's something for the kids, but if the adults want to get on the bandwagon, more power to them."

No, more power to you, Booker, as he not only loves what he's doing for a living, he's also very aware of his actions both on the TV screen and in the ring. He doesn't want to lead any child or fan in the wrong direction. He knows that his actions can very well be repeated by anyone taking in the show, and that sometimes kids don't even know they're doing wrong. They're just repeating what their favorite wrestlers are doing on the mat. And for this reason, Booker T will do anything in his power to steer kids in the right direction.

"I think kids are being shortchanged these days," he explained. "Because what do they know about T&A or vulgar language?"

Booker fell into a bad crowd when he was young. Both of his parents had died by the time he was fourteen years old and he credits his brother, Stevie Ray, also a professional wrestler, with helping him get back on the right path. Unfortunately, nowadays the two can't even be in the same arena together.

Ray captured ten tag titles with his brother at his side when they formed one of the greatest tag teams of all time as the Harlem Heat. Some even go so far as to say that the Harlem Heat was the most dominant duo of all time.

Booker agrees with the statement "In my eyes, it was one of the greatest tag teams that ever lived in the 1990s."

But bad blood surfaced when Stevie took it upon himself to defend one of Booker's single's titles while T was recovering from an injury. Booker was nursing a bad knee that had been torn up by Bret Hart in a match during the 1998 Bash at the Beach, so Ray decided to step into the ring to defend what he says was not only his brother's belt, but also his honor.

After initially winning in his brother's place, Ray again went out and acted as if the title were his own and faced other wrestlers with Booker's title on the line. While T was stewing over his sibling's actions, he tried not to let these incidents come between him and his brother, even after Ray lost the belt and title to Chris Jericho. On this occasion, Ray claimed that Booker gave him the "power of attorney" to defend his title, but as it turned out, Stevie certainly didn't have the power to defeat Jericho, and it looked as though he was going to need an attorney when it was over. But Booker forgave his brother.

With his knee all healed up, Booker was ready to return to the ring. He had no qualms about pairing up with his tag partner again. The two would capture three more tag titles in 1999, but when 2000 came around Harlem really heated up. Stevie became pissed at his brother for working with Midnight, a beautiful young lady who was blessed with strength, athleticism, and good looks. So, the jealous brother formed an alliance with another wrestler, Big T, and they began parading around as the new Harlem Heat. Needless to say, this didn't sit well with Booker, who now claims he's done with his brother for good. While it's a shame that this had to happen to such a good guy, it was all for the better.

Stevie Ray and Harlem Heat were holding Booker back. He was now free to do what he was best at: kicking ass one-on-one. In no time, he would sit atop the wrestling world holding the coveted world championship belt.

On July 9, 2000, in Daytona Beach, Florida, Booker defeated Jeff Jarrett to garner his first WCW world heavyweight championship title. This night not only proved that nice guys don't always finish last, but more importantly, Booker T was alive and well on the singles circuit, ready to kick some serious butt!

Big Boss Man

Here's a wrestler who not only intimidates with his size, but if you don't watch out, Ray Traylor, a.k.a. the Big Boss Man, might also work you over with his nightstick. The former real-life prison guard from Cobb County, Georgia, has been on the side of both good and

Howard Kernats

evil in his career. He has defended the honor of his boss, Vince McMahon, from Steve Austin and The Undertaker at one time and has also been a four-time holder of the Hardcore title.

The 6-foot-6, 315-pound grappler has even worn the tag-team belt in his career. In December 1998, the big guy held the title with his ring partner, Ken Shamrock, as they won the belts from the New Age Outlaws in Tacoma, Washington.

Known for his Boss Man Slam, the big, bad grappler has made his presence known ever since he gave up working at the prisons full-time in Georgia for the glory of the ring. There is no limit to the torture he will put his opponent through. He once fed Al Snow his own dog, and he also once dragged the casket of The Big Show's father behind a moving car.

Before coming to the WWF in the 1990s Traylor wrestled in the WCW under the ring name of Big Bubba Rogers, where he was the imposing bodyguard of Jim Cornette. He has also wrestled under his real name, as well as the moniker of Guardian Angel.

But no matter the name or opponent, one thing is for certain, when Boss Man is in the house, Big things are going to happen.

D'Lo Brown

This man literally has the brains and brawn to be whatever he wants to be in life and D'Lo Brown chose to be a professional wrestler. Besides being one of the most technically skilled grapplers in the game, D'Lo (a.k.a. A. C. Connor) is also a graduate of the University of Maine, where he received his bachelor's degree in accounting. When he's not taxing his opponent in the ring, this certified public accountant is out in the business world filing tax returns for his clients.

Brown got his start in the World Wrestling Federation when Faarooq recruited him to be a bodyguard for the Nation of Domination. He quickly earned a name for himself in the WWF in the tag ranks, but he impressed the viewers and the powers-that-be even more on the singles circuit.

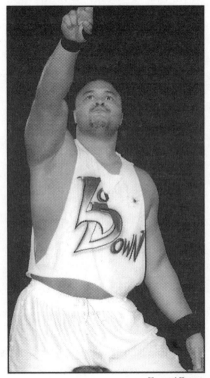

Howard Kernats

On July 14, 1998, D'Lo made the biggest impression of all on the federation when he beat Triple H for his first WWF title. Brown squared off against the two-time European champion on a hot night in July in Binghamton, New York, and beat Triple H to become the new

37

European title holder. Since that victory, D'Lo has gone on to win the belt an impressive four more times. He has also garnered the WWF's Intercontinental championship in his short time with the federation.

Wrestling in an age where aerial moves almost have to be a part of your repertoire, Brown doesn't disappoint. Even though he weighs in at 275 pounds, the 6-foot-3 grappler can flat out fly! His finishing move, known as the 'Lo Down, is a version of the Frog Splash, which happens to be one of the most stunning aerial maneuvers around.

The Demon

Talk about art imitating life— or wrestling, in this case. The Demon character, which Dale Torborg portrays in the ring, hits really close to home for the WCW superstar. The Demon persona is based on the Gene Simmons character of the super-famous rock group KISS, whom Torborg not only grew up listening to, but also dressed up as on occasion.

As early as the age of five, Torborg admired the legendary rock group, especially their fire-breathing guitarist Simmons. He first came into contact with the group when his older brother

Howard Kernats

brought home the KISS *Destroyer* album and the young Torborg noticed their cool look on the album cover.

"I remember looking at the cover of the album before I even listened to it and thinking 'These guys are cool as hell.' Then I started listening to it, and I got hooked on the music," Torborg told *WCW Magazine* in their September 2000 issue.

The youngster not only grew up a KISS fan, but he was also the son of Major League Baseball player Jeff Torborg, who played for both the Los Angles Dodgers and the California Angels. So becoming a pro wrestler didn't even cross his mind until the day he met Hulk Hogan on an airplane to sunny Florida. The Hulkster put the bug in Torborg's head that he had the size and athleticism to give pro grappling a try, and when his pro baseball career came to a sudden halt due to an eye injury, he remembered Hogan's kind words.

Torborg began training in Tampa under the tutelage of former WWF and WCW wrestler The Warlord. He wrestled on the indy circuit in both Florida and Georgia, as well as the AWF, until he was discovered by WCW talent manager J. J. Dillon in 1997.

Dillon enrolled Torborg at the WCW Power Plant in Atlanta, where he honed his skills for six months before making his federation debut. He bounced around on the circuit under several other ring names, but came into his own in 1999, when he was approached about doing The Demon role.

The now-scary grappler worked his way up the WCW ladder via his dark-warrior character and has crossed paths with another monster-of-a-wrestler—Vampiro. To say that their rivalry has been on fire is an understatement. But what's not an understatement is The Demon's presence in the federation. He should remain on fire for a long time to come.

Diamond Dallas Page

The Rock isn't the only people's champion in wrestling these days. Grappling fans are pretty fond of another warrior, and that's Diamond Dallas Page.

Page is a true-to-life wrestling success story as he's climbed his way up through the wrestling ranks from the very bottom to the very top. Although he didn't physically wrestle in the ring until 1991 with World Championship Wrestling, he was involved in the mat antics since 1988, when he was the manager of a duo called Badd Company (Paul Diamond and Pat Tanaka) in the AWA. Before moving on to Florida Championship

Howard Kernats

Wrestling, Page would guide his team to the World Tag Team title.

While with FCW, the 6-foot-5, New Jersey native not only continued managing, he also tried his luck at color commentating. He found success on both stages, being respected by his fellow wrestlers, which included Johnny Ace, Bam Bam Bigelow, and Dick Slater and also teaming at ringside with the legendary announcer Gordon Solie.

In 1991 DDP got the call from the WCW to come onboard as a manager for a tag team known as The Freebirds, and he immediately accepted. By February of 1991, The Freebirds (Michael Hayes and

Jimmy Garvin) were wearing championship gold around their waists and they had only Page to thank. Before stepping between the ropes himself, he took another young stud under his wing in Diamond Studd (Scott Hall) and showed him the ropes.

Being the competitor that he was, DDP could no longer be content with being so close yet so far from the action, so he turned over a new page in his career and entered the ring as a full-time grappler later in 1991. He quickly became popular on the mat scene and enjoyed being associated with beautiful people such as Vinnie Vegas (Kevin Nash), Scotty Flamingo (Raven), and of course his "Diamond Dolls," several gorgeous women who would escort Dallas to the ring. One of these beautiful gals, Kimberly Falkenberg, became his one and only in real life, as the two wrestling personalities were married a short time after meeting.

Although he took the scenic route getting inside the squared circle action, Page proved that he had what it took to take on the best of the best. Whether he was wrestling as a cigar-smoking scoundrel or battling the federation's nasty boys, the nWo, the former manager never disappointed his audience while in the ring. He had memorable feuds with Goldberg, Ric Flair, and Randy "Macho Man" Savage. He also teamed with Karl Malone and Jay Leno at one time and grappled against the NBA's bad boy, Dennis Rodman.

Page has made all his opponents "feel the bang" at one time or another and has a pretty good trail of championship gold to back up his efforts. The seven-time title winner has won the WCW World Heavyweight title twice, the WCW U.S. title twice, the tag-team belt twice, and the TV title once in his career. Not bad for someone who started on the outside looking in as a manager.

The former high school football and basketball standout is all about overcoming the odds in his life. Not only did he climb the ladder in the wrestling world, but he was also able to overcome dyslexia to conquer his fear of reading as a child. He and his wife, Kimberly, are very active in his charity, Bang It Out for Books, which helps kids fight illiteracy and promotes reading.

This is a man, good or bad, who will make you take notice. "You love me [or] you hate me, [but] you'll never forget me," Page says.

True, how true.

Disco Inferno

Who says disco is dead? It's very much alive and well in the form of WCW superstar Disco Inferno. Whether you catch him as Disco Inferno or Disqo, it doesn't really matter as this cool, gold-chain-wearing grappler marches to the beat of his own drum—or bad seventies music in his case.

The 6-foot-1, 240-pound wrestler has danced his way to three wrestling titles in his career, with one coming in the WCW cruiserweight ranks. In what was a bit of a change for the Italian Stallion, he got to wear gold around his waist instead of around his neck when he beat Alex Wright on September 22, 1997, in Salt Lake City, Utah, for the WCW TV title. More than a month later, on November 3, he lost the strap to Saturn, but regained the title on December 8.

Howard Kernats

His next claim to fame, besides his dancing, came on October 4, 1999, when he won the cruiserweight title from Psicosis in Kansas City, Missouri. He then hooked on with his 'fella Italians, The Mamalukes, and guided them all the way to the top of the tag ranks. The two thugs from Brooklyn notched the belts on January 19, 2000, from David Flair and Crowbar in Evansville, Indiana, under the watchful eyes of Disco.

Inferno, a.k.a. Glen Gilbertti, is a crowd favorite every time he enters the ring, entertaining the fans with his extravagant, chest revealing costumes, and his John Travolta–like gyrations. Even though his hair barely moves during his matches, don't let that fool you. This grappler can throw down with the best of 'em with moves such as the Chartbuster and Last Dance up his polyester shirtsleeves.

When it comes to Disco Inferno, only three things are certain: first, that he has a copy of the *Saturday Night Fever* and *Bee Gees Greatest Hits* CDs, second, that he'll give you a sizzling performance every time out on the wrestling floor, and third, that he'll be the next host of *Dance Fever* when the show comes back on the tube.

Shane Douglas

Howard Kernats

Shane Douglas, a.k.a. Troy Martin, has played both a babyface and heel in his career so far, and without a doubt he's a much better heel. The Pittsburgh, Pennsylvania, native started out his career under the supervision of wrestling legend Dominic DeNucci, from whom he learned all about the sport along with Mick Foley and the late Brian Hildebrand.

The training under DeNucci would pay off, as Douglas made his pro debut in November 1983. During the 1980s he made a name for himself in his first time around in the NWA (today known as the WCW) as a member of The Dynamic Dudes with Johnny Ace. A tandem that would have classic battles with The Midnight Express.

He grew frustrated in his role with the promotion at that time and left the federation, only to return to bigger and better things several years later. Douglas came back to a newly titled federation (WCW) and a new tag partner, the legendary Ricky Steamboat. In no time the duo just clicked and began taking on any and all who wanted a piece of them.

On November 18, 1992, Douglas and Steamboat defeated Barry Windham and Dustin Rhodes for the federation's tag-team title. The tandem would also clash with another fearless twosome, The Hollywood Blondes (Steve Williams, today known as "Stone Cold" Steve Austin, and Brian Pillman). Their matches were so great that on some occasions they were moved up to the main event because of the rush they would give the crowd. This in itself was a major accomplishment as tag matches are very rarely, if ever, used as the main drawing cards.

But again, Douglas would become frustrated with the promotion and left the WCW to pursue a grappling career with the more extreme brand of wrestling that ECW was offering. This would play a major role in his development as a wrestler, because he not only learned new skills in the ring, but, more important, he learned how to be a heel.

While with ECW, Douglas went from being a good technical wrestler to one who had a full arsenal that could be utilized for brawling. Two of the most important additions to his game were his now convincing mic skills and his deadly finisher, known as the Pittsburgh Plunge.

After putting in his time with ECW, he again returned to the WCW, where he plies his trade today. The Franchise character has gone over really well with the fans, and Douglas enjoys every bit of playing this badass role for the audience.

When asked in an interview with scoopswrestling.com which role he prefers to play, heel or face, Douglas had this to say: "Absolutely a heel. The Franchise character is a heel. He's an asshole. He's the dark arrogant side of everybody that they try to keep under wraps. Troy Martin just lets him out. He's the guy that is good at what he does and knows it. If he lived next door he'd smack you in the face before he'd cut the grass. The Franchise doesn't play well to a babyface. After playing him for seven years, my tendencies in the ring are heelish. Even when Steamboat and I were the babyface tag champions, Bill Watts used to say 'damn, your character is such a heel!' I was The Franchise even before The Franchise."

There you have it . . . right from the mouth of a heel!

The Dudley Boyz

Howard Kernats

After being in the World Wrestling Federation for just a little over a year, The Dudley Boyz have skyrocketed to the top of not only the tag-team ranks in terms of popularity, but more impressively, up the personality ladder, where they get just about the same thunderous pop from the crowd as a solo personality. Aside from their in-ring accomplishments, this in itself is an unbelievable achievement when you look at the WWF's talent roster and see such names as The Rock, "Stone Cold" Steve Austin, and Triple H.

In an interview for *The Long Islander* newspaper last May, Buh Buh Ray Dudley had this to say about their lightning-quick rise to the top: "There hasn't been a tag team in a very long time that has ever been in that upper-five percentile when it comes to the show and everything that goes on. But when it comes to all the guys that are there, just to be in that upper-five percentile as a tag team, be in main event status and everything every night. That's what we're looking to do. We're looking to crack the upper echelon of the company."

And crack they do!

One of the main draws of their matches is how they dispose of their opponents. One of their most popular gimmicks is to take their helpless foes and drive them through wooden tables, a feat they call "getting wood"!

When it comes to "getting wood" no one is safe. No superstars are passed over. No executives. Not even the ladies of the federation! As a matter of fact, when the duo first broke into the WWF they plowed one of the game's greatest female wrestlers, Mae Young, who was also seventy-eight-years old at the time, through a table. This caused not only a hush over the crowd, but it also left the powers-that-be scratching their heads, wondering if these two were a cheeseburger short of a happy meal!

Pics Pix

But this act wasn't new to the terrible twosome. They made a practice of it during their time at Extreme Championship Wrestling, when on one occasion they "broke the neck" of one of the federation's beauties, Beulah McGillicutty.

Before coming to the WWF, The Dudley Boyz, Buh Buh Ray and D-Von, perfected their gameplan on the mats of ECW in Philadelphia, Pennsylvania.

Even though Buh Buh Ray claims to be from Dudleyville, USA, he entered the ECW by way of Long Island, New York. The 6-foot-4, 275-pound, Coke-bottle–eyeglass-wearing wrestler was born Mark Lomonica on July 7, 1971, and ever since he could remember, he'd wanted to become a pro wrestler.

He signed on with the House of Hardcore in New York, the main wrestling training plant for ECWers, and it was there that he learned how to grapple. When the federation came calling, they placed him with a clan known as The Dudleys. In its early stages, the team was

Triple H's role in "the game" is being the
biggest heel in wrestling.

Eddie Guerrero and his "Mamacita," Chyna, always
generate "Latino Heat" inside the ring.

The Dudley Boyz, D-Von and Buh Buh Ray, love turning the tables on their opponents.

Scotty Too Hotty and Grand Master Sexay
are just "Too Cool" for words!

Opponents better beware when Rikishi
starts backing that thang up!

Howard Kernats

Diamond Dallas Page, Jeff Jarrett, and The Demon all have a certain feel when they step into the ring. DDP makes his foes feel the bang, while Double J makes his opponents feel the music. The Demon simply makes 'em feel the heat.

Howard Kernats

Howard Kernats

Russell Turiak

Sting may have recovered from the burns received at the Human Inferno match, but he has yet to recover from wanting revenge on the mega-heel Vampiro.

Russell Turiak

Kevin Nash is a wrestler who does what he
wants when he wants!

When Goldberg turned heel on June 11, 2000, fans knew it couldn't last for long—he is truly a super hero at heart!

not what it is today. The Dudleys were a large clan of wrestlers from all walks of life, who were not only all from Dudleyville, USA, but they all were also supposed to be brothers, even though none of them looked alike.

While Buh Buh Ray was one of the original members, D-Von didn't come along until a short while afterward. He claimed to be from Dudleyville, USA, but in reality, he also grew up on the streets of New York—Brooklyn, in fact. The 6-foot-2, 240-pound grappler credits wrestling for keeping him in school and off the streets as a child.

Born Devon Hughes, the youngster grew up admiring Hulk Hogan and instead of hanging out on the mean streets of Flatbush, he would rush home to watch the Hulkster and his crew square off against one another.

"When I was young, you had a lot of kids, especially in my neighborhood, that were either getting killed or doing things that you weren't supposed to be doing," Hughes said in a interview with *The Long Islander* newspaper. "But my main objective was just to get home to watch wrestling. I was captivated by Hulk Hogan. I would go home to watch who was challenging him or who he was going to challenge. That kept me from wanting to be outside with the bad people. That kept me in school."

The young Brooklynite would commute to Long Island to attend John Glenn High School, where he would also star on the varsity football team. While he liked playing the gridiron sport and had thoughts of pursuing a professional career in football, his mind would always wander back to becoming a pro wrestler like his boyhood idol, Hulk Hogan.

Once he realized that was definitely the route he wanted to take, he wasted no time and, like Lomonica, joined the House of Hardcore. While being taught the tricks of the trade at Hardcore, he fell into an opportunity that would land him right in the heart of Dudleyville. ECW needed another brother to add to the clan and Hughes's trainer recommended him.

When the two decided to pair off and form a tag team, it wouldn't be long before they would wreak havoc on the rest of the federation.

They won their first belts on March 15, 1997, in Philadelphia against The Eliminators, after only being together as a duo for a short period of time. While they didn't win every bout they took part in, it didn't matter. They were making a name for themselves not only in the ECW, but all over the wrestling world. By the time the year came to an end, the new duo had two more tag titles to add to their resume.

The twosome, who were crowd-jeering heels, would run roughshod over the rest of the tag tandems in the ECW. But this in itself was no easy feat, squaring off against some mean teams such as: The Eliminators, The Gangstas, Public Enemy, and Rob Van Dam and Sabu.

But beating the tough competition wasn't their drawing card. It was their rude, crude, and violent style that kept the fans coming back for more. The Dudleys took Extreme Wrestling to another level. They went from using steel chairs on the craniums of their foes, to smashing them through one table, then two, and when that wasn't enough, they added fire to the mix and hurled their opponents through the now blazing pieces of furniture. Oh yeah, and let's not forget their lethal finishing maneuver, the 3-D, short for the Dudley Death Drop. This move happens to be one of, if not the most, devastating finishers in the business today.

After winning their eighth tag-title belt on March 26, 1999, against Balls Mahoney and Spike Dudley, the two decided that it was time to move on, and they hooked up with Vince McMahon's promotion, the WWF. Many wondered whether or not they would make it because the Connecticut-based organization was not as violent as the Philly-based one, but the Boyz proved all the naysayers wrong.

While, yes, their act was violent and borderline sadistic, the tandem didn't win a record eight tag championships in the ECW just on their antics alone. They'll be the first to admit that they competed in some of the most bloody, violent, and dangerous matches ever, but the tag powerhouses can flat-out wrestle. Buh Buh Ray and D-Von combine raw, physical power with some great technical moves in the ring. While they aren't one of the high-flying duos like The Hardy Boyz or Edge & Christian, they don't have to be in order to be successful. Their unique style of grappling is what got them to where they are today.

The Dudleys have made it in the WWF not only on their table-breaking skills, but also on their hard work. The team is always looking for ways to add to their showmanship. They came into the federation and worked their way from the bottom on up. There have been several defining moments so far in their career, one being winning their first WWF tag straps from the New Age Outlaws on February 27, 2000, in Hartford, Connecticut. But none could compare to their three-way ladder matches with The Hardy Boyz and Edge & Christian in both WrestleMania 2000 and SummerSlam.

While the duo didn't win either match, as a matter of fact, they lost the belts to Edge & Christian at WrestleMania, they did something way more important for their careers. They earned the respect of the fans, who are the real make-or-breakers in the business.

The Dudleys proved that they are for real and can compete with anyone thrown their way, so the rest of the federation should be aware that "Thou shall not mess with the Dudleys!"

Edge & Christian

Edge & Christian can not only compete with the best of 'em on the tag circuit, these two young guns also have what it takes to be successful in the singles ranks.

In 1999, Edge, who is a native of Canada, won the Intercontinental Championship in stunning fashion as he garnered the belt in his home-town of Toronto in a hard-fought battle at a sold-out SkyDome on July 24 over Jeff Jarrett.

The long-haired, sunglasses-wearing wrestler, whose real name is Adam Copeland, was discovered by WWF executive Carl DeMarco wrestling on the Canadian coast. DeMarco liked the way the youngster wrestled—using his quickness along with various acrobatic maneuvers that his opponents couldn't match.

He invited the young Copeland for a trial match against a veteran mat-man, Bob Holly, and the inexperienced grappler held his own against the experienced WWFer. By putting on a good performance against Holly, Copeland was signed to a deal by DeMarco. He imme-diately hooked up with The Undertaker and went over to the dark side as part of the Ministry of Darkness.

Most of his career he has been a mysterious grappler, living life according to his new WWF ring name—on the edge. The popular wres-tler likes to finish off his foes with his Downward Spiral maneuver.

Christian, Copeland's partner in crime, also found success on the singles circuit before he teamed up with Edge to form one of today's best tag teams.

On October 18, 1998, the up-and-coming grappler won his first WWF gold in Chicago, Illinois, when he grabbed hold of the light heavyweight title over Taka Michinoku. This was quite a feat for Christian, real name Christian Cage, who had only made his pro wrestling debut three years earlier. He also won the ECWA Heavyweight title in his career, but that win came before his more impressive WWF victory.

Cage, also a native of Canada, had trained under Ron Hutchinson at Sully's Gym in Toronto before hitting the pro circuits. During the summer of 1997, he worked alongside his future WWF tag partner, Copeland, as they took on Don Callis and Rick Martel at independent shows.

Christian, like Edge, mainly got his push through his dark side associations. He was also part of the Ministry of Darkness with Edge, The Undertaker, and Gangrel. Gangrel then broke away from the Ministry and took the two of them with him into an even darker side of the wrestling world, forming a hell-raising trio called The Brood.

But once the two teamed up against the other duos in the federation, there was no keeping them down. Edge & Christian brought a certain flare to the arena. They combined good looks with great technique to go along with their amazing aerial acrobatics. They would not only keep the crowd cheering, they would, more important, keep them on the edge of their seats, awaiting their next daring move.

Howard Kernats

The duo came into their own in 1999, when they combined with The Hardy Boyz in one of the most memorable tag matches ever! On October 17, 1999, the four very talented wrestlers squared off in a ladder match on a Pay-Per-View event entitled No Mercy that more than lived up to its billing.

Even though they lost the contest, they had proved not only to everyone watching, but more important the WWF officials, that they were ready to wear some tag gold around their waists. On April 2, 2000, at WrestleMania, the young hopefuls got their wish. But sometimes you should watch what you wish for because they not only had to face The Hardy Boyz on this night, but also the sadistic Dudley Boyz, who were the reigning champs, in a three-way ladder match.

When all was said and done in the free-for-all brawl, Edge & Christian would walk away with their first WWF tag championship. They would lose the title in a little less than a month to Too Cool, but would take it back in a rematch three weeks later on June 25 and reclaim their hold on the belts.

At SummerSlam, the three teams that had squared off at WrestleMania 2000 met again in a ladder match and the action was nonstop table-breaking, ladder-fighting, body-pounding excitement. Both The Dudley Boyz and The Hardy Boyz tried to get hold of the belts from atop the ladder, but Edge & Christian would again walk away victorious with the title straps still theirs.

Edge & Christian no longer wrestle on the dark side these days having changed their image to one that is more "fan friendly," posing for photo ops whenever possible. This tandem has brought excitement back to the tag scene and there's no telling what lies ahead for this fabulous twosome.

Faarooq

Faarooq, a.k.a. Ron Simmons, is a wrestler who has been both a heel and a hero in his career, but unlike some of his co-workers, he truly loves the hero role away from the ring. He is a veteran grappler who has had his share of "golden days" between the ropes, and who goes out of his way to show young wrestlers the ropes when they need advice.

"When I leave this profession, I want to be able to say that I took the time to help other guys like I was helped," Faarooq said in an interview for *Raw Magazine*'s March

2000 issue. "What else can I accomplish? Everybody wants to be a champion, of course. But I've been one. Now, it's not about having a belt. The satisfaction comes with seeing the success of this profession and with having it respected."

Speaking of respect, Simmons has plenty of it in and around the wrestling circuit. He has won two tag-team championships and is also a former WCW World Heavyweight champion, the first African-American grappler in any major professional federation to ever have been able to stake that claim.

Faarooq has been a brawler and leader ever since he first came onto the wrestling scene in 1996 after his days on the football field were through. He was a gridiron standout at Florida State University, where his jersey number was retired, but his love of one-on-one physical competition led him to the world of pro wrestling.

Simmons is best known for forming a heel group known as The Nation of Domination, whose main purpose in the WWF was to monitor the careers of minority superstars within the federation who they claimed were being "suppressed." But under his leadership, this group did more than monitor. The Nation created all kinds of "heel heat" and went to war on many occasions with any and all who they felt were standing in their way.

Today, Faarooq is part of another protection agency, the Acolyte Protection Agency, which he founded with Bradshaw. Together, they "offer" protection to any federation superstar who has the money for the APA's services. Faarooq and Bradshaw are two of the meanest S.O.B.s in the WWF, but they also like to have their fun.

When they're not bashing heads or "protecting" their colleagues, they can be found smoking cigars, drinking beer, and playing cards. But a word to the wise: don't interrupt them when they're in the middle of a game. You may get more than you bargained for with these two vicious grapplers.

When he isn't playing cards, smoking cigars, drinking beer, or providing protection, Simmons can be found doling out advice to the young guns in the organization.

"We've got a lot of young guys here," he said. "There's a lot of things that I can teach them. Lots of guys look up to me for advice and watch me to learn things."

And when asked if he enjoys playing the role of "role model" to these youngsters, he had this to say: "I enjoy the role I'm in now. People helped me along the way; now it's my turn to give back."

David Flair

There's only one wrestler who plays the role of a bigger heel outside the ring than he is when he's between the ropes, and that's David Flair. This son of a rich father has an eye for the gals just like dear old dad. The young Flair has the unfortunate privilege to try and follow in his dad's footsteps not only as a top-notch wrestler, but also as a ladies' man.

In the little time he has been on the World Championship Wrestling circuit, he has managed to hook up with some of the most beautiful babes in the business.

Howard Kernats

And the Minneapolis native proved that he will stop at nothing in order to be with the lovely lady of his choice. At one time he turned on his father, Ric, to not only team with Hulk Hogan and Kevin Nash, but to also be closer to sexy Torrie Wilson. Flair used his, well, flair to get the easy-on-the-eyes Wilson to become his valet.

He then reunited with his father not to rebuild the bridges that had been burned in the past, but to get hold of the U.S. title, which his dad literally handed to him. After picking up the belt, he decided it was time to do another kind of picking up, and he set his sights on the delightful Daffney. The blond bomber would not only be successful in getting

Daffney to become his valet, he would charm his way into her heart, and she would eventually become his fiancée.

Along the way, Flair also nabbed the tag title as he paired up with Crowbar in Greenville, South Carolina, on January 3, 2000. These partnerships didn't last long as Flair not only grew tired of Daffney, but also Crowbar. He broke up the tag partnership with his fellow title holder and cheated on Daffney with Ms. Hancock in the process.

Will he ever give up this crazy lifestyle of babes and betrayal? It's highly unlikely as he's the son of a wrestler who has the reputation as a stylin' and profilin' wrestler and ladies' man. And you know what they say: the apple doesn't fall far from the tree.

Ric Flair

Ric Flair is a wrestler that falls into a unique category: despised by many and loved by most. The Minnesota native can be considered way ahead of his time as an in-ring performer, fitting right into the mold of the modern-day wrestler of being great on the mic as well as in the ring.

The stylin' and profilin' grappler has the ability to do what few heels have been able to do in the past, and that's being a crowd and federation favorite. Most wrestling heels usually live up to their names, being loudly booed and hated by the fans. Not Flair. He has a charisma in the ring that is second to none. He has wheeled, dealed, and jet-setted his way right to the top of the wrestling world ever since he first graced the mat industry with his pretty-boy face in 1972.

Howard Kernats

He has a certain "flair" on the mat. From his sparkling robes to his strutting into the ring to the assortment of beautiful women on his arms, Flair has it all and has done it all in the business. He is considered by some to be the best all-around wrestler to ever grace the mat. This fact can't be argued when you look at Flair's track record: a fifteen-time world heavyweight champion who also has thirty-three other various titles to his credit.

"Nature Boy" has certainly lived up to his "to be The Man, you have to beat The Man" saying, since he has taken on any and all who

have come his way during a long career. Flair has battled the top dogs
in wrestling, including Hulk Hogan, Sting, Wahoo McDaniel, Ricky
Steamboat, Lex Luger, and Harley Race. Again, Flair was ahead of his
time when he formed a wrestling faction known as the Four Horsemen
before gangs like D-X or the nWo were even thought of. He joined
alliances with Tully Blanchard, and Ole and Arn Anderson to form
wrestling's first-ever clique.

The Horsemen has had many prominent grapplers as members at
one time or another. Some of the wrestlers who were a part of the group
have been: Flair, Arn Anderson (the only member in every incarnation),
Tully Blanchard, Ole Anderson, Lex Luger, Barry Windham, Sting, Sid
Vicious, Paul Roma, Chris Benoit, Brian Pillman, Steve McMichael,
Curt Hennig, and Dean Malenko.

Flair has not only been able to survive for almost thirty years in a
rough and tumble business; he has been able to thrive. He made his
ring debut on December 10, 1972, against George "Scrap Iron" Gadaski
and has never looked back.

Well, maybe just once.

On October 4, 1975, Flair's life and career almost came to an abrupt
end. The pro wrestler was involved in an airplane crash and suffered a
broken back when the Cessna 310 he was riding in crashed near Wil-
mington, North Carolina. Also on the plane with him that unlucky night
was Johnny Valentine and Bob Bruggers. It was thought that the blond-
haired, blue-eyed grappler's wrestling days were over, but surprisingly,
Flair was back in the ring in less than a year.

As a matter of fact, Flair would win his first title only seven months
after the crash. On May 24, 1976, he defeated Wahoo McDaniel in
Charlotte, North Carolina, to win the Mid-Atlantic Heavyweight title.
And seven months after that he won his first world title. On December
25, 1976, Flair teamed with Greg Valentine to defeat NWA World tag
team champions Gene and Ole Anderson in Greensboro, North Carolina, to become the new tag titleholder along with Valentine.

He has been a superstar in both of the big two federations over the
course of his career.

He made his debut with the World Wrestling Federation on September 10, 1991, when he wrestled Jim Powers in a bout, forcing him to submit to his lethal Figure-Four leglock hold in Cornwall, Ontario. He won his first federation title on January 19, 1992, at the Royal Rumble in Albany, New York.

1991 would also be a memorable year in the history of wrestling as two of the all-time greats, Flair and Hulk Hogan, would square off for the first time. Flair would defeat his hulking foe on this night in Dayton, Ohio, much to the chagrin of Hogan and the crowd.

"Slick Ric" is not only popular here in the States; he has wrestled all over the world during his career and squared off against some of the greatest wrestlers in the world. In one instance, March 21, 1991, he squared off in a New Japan/WCW event held in Tokyo that drew over 64,000 fans to the Tokyo Dome. Flair would face IWGP (International Wrestling Grand Prix) heavyweight champ Tatsumi Fujinami in the main event and lose. But the American champion got his revenge on his foreign foe back home in the States in May 1991 when he beat Fujinami in a bout in St. Petersburg, Florida.

He is one of five men to ever hold the WWF and NWA/WCW World titles. The other greats are Buddy Rogers, Hulk Hogan, Randy Savage, and Kevin Nash. While he may not be the most talented wrestler ever, the man knows how to get the job done when he steps through the ropes. Flair has caused some havoc along the way; winning a good share of matches and belts. Ultimately, though, his image is one that can be copied but never duplicated, as Flair is truly one of a kind.

This snazzy-dressing athlete is a true mat technician, who can beat his opponent in so many ways with the ability to either smash in his opponents' heads or get inside them in order to come away with the victory. His durability is also a major achievement as so many wrestlers have come and gone over the years, because they can't stand the combination of the grueling travel schedule along with the insanely physical matches.

But Flair has stood the test of time and has consistently defied the odds.

Mick Foley

Howard Kernats

What do you call a wrestler who has four distinct wrestling personalities? Is he a heel? Is he a hero? How about Sybil? Well, when it comes to Mick Foley, the term "crowd favorite" is the most fitting answer. Over the course of his successful career, he's only had one thing in mind—the happiness of his fans. Whether it was as Mankind, Cactus Jack, Dude Love, or Mick Foley, the three-time WWF champion loved to hear the roar of the crowd. He got off on giving them their money's worth and more—even if it meant he had to put himself in harm's way.

This is a very rare practice not only in professional wrestling, but any kind of entertainment these days. Most wrestlers or entertainers are usually only interested in two things—the championship title or the money. They couldn't give a darn about the fans. They are under the impression that their interests are more important than the fans, who pay good money to see them perform. But not Foley.

He is an entertainer first and everything else second. Sure, he liked winning championships and earning cold, hard cash, but those were always secondary to the fan-loyal grappler. He hung up his wrestling boots at the conclusion of WrestleMania 2000 and has resurfaced in the World Wrestling Federation as the acting commissioner of the WWF. He now gets a chance to strike back at some of the foes he battled throughout his illustrious career. With this prestigious title, he now has the final say in most matchups and can give or take away any title or belt whenever he sees fit. That's a lot of power to give a kid from Long Island who grew up imitating his favorite ring kings.

Over fifteen years ago, a teenage Foley met up with a wrestling promoter by the name of Tommy Dee, who was doing a show at his old high school, and Dee wound up giving Foley his first job in the wrestling business as part of his ring crew. Even though he wasn't bashing in heads or his own body yet, he was able to cross paths with some famous grapplers who took a liking to the kid from New York.

Foley wound up meeting and getting tips from popular wrestlers like Bob Backlund, Larry Zbysko, Sgt. Slaughter, Rick Martel, and Dominic DeNucci. Of all these superstars, DeNucci would have the biggest impact on the future hard-core wrestler's career.

In his spare time between matches, DeNucci would not only show him moves and how to take bumps in the ring, he would personally invite Foley to his wrestling training school in Pittsburgh. Even though Foley was in college at the time, he decided to take Dominic up on this offer—traveling over 400 miles each weekend to get there—because there was nothing that he wanted out of life more than to become a professional wrestler.

On June 24, 1986, he made his ring debut against another DeNucci student, Kurt Kaufman, in Clarksburg, West Virginia. Kaufman, who had some pro experience from his time on the indy circuit, defeated the inexperienced Foley in the ring on that night, but it didn't matter to the newcomer as he was on his way to becoming a full-time grappler.

Foley would ply his trade all over the wrestling world. Wherever they needed a 6-foot-2, 297-pound, out-of-shape grappler he was there. That's right. Out of shape. But this was the beauty of Mick Foley. He came into the wrestling world out of shape, and went out the same way, but what he did in-between is what wrestling fans will never forget.

He bounced around as not only different characters, but also in

different federations. At one time or another he has wrestled for the
IWA, CWA, UWF, ECW, WCW, and the WWF. You name the federation and Foley has been there. Hell, it's a good bet that he probably
broke a bone or two there also.

In his mat history, Foley has suffered six concussions, a broken jaw,
a broken nose (twice), a broken cheekbone, a broken left thumb, a broken right wrist, two-thirds of his left ear lost, a torn abdomen, four
front teeth knocked out, a broken toe, both shoulders dislocated, second
degree burns, broken ribs, and he has over 325 body stitches to his
credit.

But he'll be the first one to tell you that it was all worth it. Yeah,
he may have suffered a bit along the way, but he was able to make a
living doing what he loved and that was entertaining the crowd as a pro
wrestler. The reason the fans have grown so fond of Foley over the
years is because they grew to know that there wasn't anything he
wouldn't do to keep them happy.

One of the first instances Foley went above and beyond for the
crowd was in March 1994 in an overseas match against Vader. He lost
one of his ear lobes in the ring in Germany during a bout against the
round wrestler. Vader caught Foley's head between the top and middle
ropes, and when Foley tried to free himself, he ripped off part of his
left ear and did some damage to the right lobe as well. But being the
showman that he was, he continued to wrestle and wound up losing not
only his ear, but the match as well.

Another memorable matchup occurred in 1995, at the IWA's Death
Match tournament in Japan. Even in a tourney that had everything under the sun from barbed wire, steel chairs, baseball bats, bats with
barbed wire, beds of nails, and exploding platforms, Foley would find a
way to go the extra mile and add a little something extra to the show.

After beating Terry "Bam Bam" Gordy, Leatherface, Tiger Jeet
Singh, and others on that memorable night in the King of the Death
Match tournament, he would have to face his friend Terry Funk. The
ropes would be replaced by barbed wire for the contest and there were
also exploding planks that were set to go off during the final match. Oh,

yeah, I left out the best detail. There was a firebomb set to go off and leave the ring in a fiery mess.

Well, as the two warriors beat each other to a bloody pulp, something went wrong. The explosion went bad and let out nothing but a puff of smoke. You would think that the wrestlers would have been relieved, but not Foley. Seeing how disappointed the fans were, he took it upon himself to turn up the heat. He threw a ladder into the ring and the two went at each other at an even more intense pace. This was when most of the injuries occurred to the two matsmen, but Foley didn't care. He just wanted to see his fans smiling, even though he felt like crying. The payback was worth it for him, but the paycheck left a lot to be desired.

"I had seven stitches in my hand, fourteen behind this ear, twelve in my head, and seven over my eye, as well as second degree burns. For that I got three hundred dollars," Foley said in an interview with *SLAM Wrestling*. "[But] I think there are enough people out there who understand what I do to make it worthwhile."

But he rationalized his in-ring behavior by having several different characters who wrestled in different manners. While he mostly liked to grapple as Mankind or Cactus Jack, who thrived on wrestling with a no-holds-barred, kamikaze, death-defying, neck-breaking, table-crashing style, there was also his Dude Love character who was more smooth within the ropes. This was a good change for him and allowed his body to rest and recuperate from all the vicious and devastating bumps and bruises he would endure over the course of his career.

But his hard-core fans didn't take a liking to this toned-down Foley character. They were accusing him of selling out and these words were stinging the crowd-pleasing performer, who always had the fans' best interests in mind, more than any bump he took in the squared circle.

"The Dude is good and should not be overlooked, because he taught me that you don't necessarily have to be in pain to entertain an audience," Foley said. "The hard-core wrestling fans can say what they want, but the fact is The Dude entertained a lot of people last year and didn't get hurt."

But whether Foley was a heel or hero in the ring, it didn't matter to his true fans. They knew he would give them everything he had in the tank that night and more. Foley wasn't one to leave anything in the locker room. Just ask any wrestler who stood across from him on the canvas for a match. Ask "Stone Cold" Steve Austin. Ask Sting. Ask Triple H. Ask The Rock. Ask Vader. Ask The Undertaker. Ask the Steiner brothers, Rick and Scott.

I'm sure all of them would tell you that Mick Foley was one of the best entertainers to ever set foot in a ring. They will say that this dude really knew how to wrestle and knew what the fans wanted! This is why Foley is so good in his WWF commissioner's role. He not only understands the industry from the wrestler's side, but more important he also has his finger on the pulse of wrestling fans everywhere.

Goldberg

On June 11, 2000, the unthinkable happened. Yes, this is pro wrestling and grapplers change their gimmicks and allegiances more often than their fighting trunks, but it's no stretch to say that the entire crowd—as a matter of fact—the entire wrestling world, didn't expect Goldberg to really turn heel!

The Oklahoma native was not only one of the federation's true superstars, he was also one of their true good guys. What could've happened? What made this babyface turn villain?

Well, according to Goldberg in an interview he did in the September 2000 issue of *WCW Magazine*, he was frustrated with the way things were going in his career and felt he needed some kind of change. "I got sick and damn tired of it all," he said, "and I came back with a new attitude. Hell hath no fury anymore."

He sure did come back with a new attitude! The Tulsa Tornado swept through the Baltimore Civic Center on that June night at The Great American Bash and took his frustrations out on poor, unsuspecting Kevin Nash. Upon his return to action a few weeks earlier from a career-threatening arm injury that had kept him out of action for several months, Goldberg had been bonding with Nash.

The heel-turning event occurred when Big Sexy was involved in a World Championship title match with "The Chosen One" Jeff Jarrett. After Nash had jackknife-powerbombed Jarrett for the second time, the Goldberg monster truck plowed into the arena.

The bald-headed grappler exited his vehicle and made his way toward the ring and the other two superstars. Then, without warning, he climbed through the ropes and crouched, readying himself for the Spear.

The stunned crowd definitely thought that Goldberg was going to take out Double J, but in heel-like manner, he took out Nash.

After nailing Nash, he tells Jarrett to make the cover and, on cue, Jarrett gets the pin and win to retain his title. After referee Mickey Jay counted Nash out, Goldberg stood in center ring and stared down on the fallen Nash. Then, to make matters worse and even more interesting, Eric Bischoff and Vince Russo climbed out of Goldberg's truck and walked to the squared circle. They gingerly approached their new heel, and after a tense moment, the three embraced, solidifying Goldberg as an official member of the WCW's New Blood.

If you thought the embrace and Goldberg's turning heel to be shocking, what about the crowd's reaction to this crazy turn of events? In unbelievable fashion, the arena erupted into loud chants of "Goldberg sucks! Goldberg sucks!"

But, the personality change wouldn't last too long for the ex–pro football player. The combination of the timing of having Goldberg turn

Howard Kernats

bad and his not liking his new role led the WCW to rethink their actions and allow Goldberg to resurface as his old self a few weeks later.

"It was hard for me because here I was making speeches to these kids and doing the things I do with charities during the day and then at night I was running those same kind of people down in the ring," Goldberg explained. "Yeah, it's just a character, but for some of the kids it's hard to understand."

Spoken like the true good guy that he is.

Even though WCW was looking for an angle that would help propel them back up in the ratings war with the WWF, having their biggest star/good guy turn evil in the prime of his career just defied wrestling logic.

Yes, history shows that wrestlers have been able to make the transition from good guy to bad guy and not lose an ounce of popularity, but that usually occurred when the star's act was growing old, and he needed a change. Hulk Hogan, Andre the Giant, Bret Hart, and even Vince McMahon all have done it. But they all did it when their character's stories had run their course. Their turns from faces to heels were shocking enough to get the push they were looking for.

Goldberg's stature in the federation as a face surely outweighed that of him playing the part of a heel. His drawing power was still on the upside as a babyface and the crowd's reaction that summer night was definitely an indicator of how they wanted their hero to act in the ring.

The fans had had a long wait for his return from his arm injury and wanted to see nothing more than the Goldberg of old. They wanted back the rugged grappler who came onto the pro wrestling scene in 1997 and ran a 173–0 record before losing to Kevin Nash in a controversial match that saw Scott Hall interfere so his friend could defeat the newcomer.

But despite his success and fan support, Goldberg will be the first to admit that wrestling was not his first career choice growing up. Actually, it wasn't even an option.

"I never considered wrestling to be an option because I thought it was silly," he said. "There was no way I was going to go out in front of millions of people wearing nothing but my underwear."

Instead, the 6-foot-3, 285-pound behemoth concentrated on becoming a pro football player. He wanted nothing more than to follow in the footsteps of his boyhood idol John Matuszak, the late, great defensive lineman for the Oakland Raiders. He parlayed a good high school career into an excellent college one playing noseguard at the University of Georgia and won All-SEC honors.

His next step was the National Football League and his boyhood dream would come true when the Los Angles Rams picked him in the eleventh round of the 1990 NFL Draft.

His time with the Rams would not only be important to his football career, but it would also open up a whole new world for him—the world of professional wrestling. He experienced this through his teammate and roommate, Kevin Greene, who was a huge grappling fan.

When Goldberg's football career didn't pan out, he turned to the form of entertainment that was closest to the gridiron sport—pro wrestling. He got the bug in his head to pursue a grappling career when, by chance, he ran into Diamond Dallas Page in a club one night and then, on another occasion, ran into Sting and Lex Luger, who all suggested he give wrestling a try.

After convincing the powers-that-be that he had what it took to compete night in and night out between the ropes, he enlisted himself in the Power Plant, a wrestling training center for all WCW hopefuls. After six months of grueling training, he was ready for action.

Goldberg made his pro wrestling debut in September 1997 against a veteran midcarder named Hugh Morrus. Before the bell could even stop ringing to start the match, the former NFLer would have his opponent beat. Though Morrus was only a midcarder, this was still impressive as Goldberg took out his foe like *he* was the seasoned vet in the ring. All WCWers should have taken note of this accomplishment, as it was a sign of things to come. The lean, mean, wrecking machine was ready to take on any and all who wanted a piece of him.

This was the beginning of not only a successful match run, it was also the beginning of a title run for the rookie grappler. After only being in the federation for seven months, Goldberg would win his first title, the U.S. Heavyweight belt, on April 20, 1998, against Raven in an anything-goes match.

Although this was impressive for the first-year pro, better things and titles awaited him. Three months later in Atlanta, he would defeat the legendary Hulk Hogan to win his first World Heavyweight title.

From here on out he earned the respect of not only his fellow wrestlers, but more important, the fans, who still adore their hero to this day!

Eddie Guerrero

Pics Pix

Ever since coming over to the World Wrestling Federation in early 2000, Eddie Guerrero has generated all kinds of Latino Heat. Most of the heat has come from his association with the love of his life—Chyna.

At first, Chyna wanted no part of the Rico Suave–like wrestler. At WrestleMania 2000 in Anaheim, California, the Ninth Wonder of the World teamed up with Too Cool in a match against Guerrero, Dean Malenko, and Perry Saturn. The match started off with Scotty Too Hotty battling it out with Guerrero and Hotty getting the better of the action early and trying to get Chyna into the ring to finish off what he'd started. But when Scotty made the tag with Chyna, Eddie reached out and tagged in Malenko.

The action went back and forth between the stars with the pace fast and furious. Guerrero was able to get in a cheap shot on Chyna when she least expected it. Sexay came to her aid and suplexed Guerrero to the mat. Again the furious pace continued with Saturn and Scotty tangling up. Chyna would again be cheap shotted by Guerrero when he nailed her with a low blow. But this time she would take the "toro" by the horns. Chyna reached out and grabbed Guerrero by his family jewels and proceeded to put him in a sleeper hold and drop him to the mat for the win.

But soon enough Chyna would be warming up to his Latino Heat. She watched him, along with the rest of the wrestling audience, win the European title the next night from Chris Jericho after being in the WWF for only a few months.

SummerSlam then rolled around and Chyna and Guerrero took part in a four-way match with Val Venis and Trish Stratus for the Intercontinental strap. This was a stipulation match, where the man or woman to score a "pinfall" would be crowned the new IC champ. And when all was said and done, Chyna came away with the belt, a WWF title she was pretty familiar with.

But her reign would be ended by none other than Guerrero, who won the belt from her on September 4, 2000. From this point on however, all became rosy for the couple. To show his love for his chica, Guerrero began presenting his "Mamacita" with a dozen long-stem roses every time they entered the ring together. At Unforgiven on September 24, 2000, in Philadelphia, Chyna helped her man defend his IC title against the well-rounded wrestler Rikishi.

But whether or not Guerrero keeps his relationship going with Chyna will have no bearing on his WWF career. The El Paso native has the high-flying ability to compete with any and all in the federation as he is a risk taker from the word *go*. Whether he remains a heel or a hero is up to the writers, but the one thing that is always for certain is that Eddie Guerrero can certainly generate Latino Heat whenever he's in the ring.

The Hardy Boyz

You want action? The Hardy Boyz will give you action. You want high-flying acrobatics? They're your choice, too. You want death-defying feats? They'll give you that, also. But another thing I can also guarantee is that these two wrestlers will be fan favorites for a long time to come.

Although Jeff and Matt Hardy have already won two World Wrestling Federation Tag Team titles, that's not why they are so loved.

Pics Pix

These two North Carolina natives night after night push the wrestling envelope. They put their bodies on the line for the sake of entertaining their fans. It is not an uncommon sight for the audience to be holding their collective breath when Matt and Jeff are in the ring—or should I say above the ring?

Most recently, the Boyz won the tag title at Unforgiven in Philadelphia, Pennsylvania, on September 24, 2000, when they took on the reigning champs Edge & Christian in a steel-cage match. As always, when these four meet between the ropes, the action was nonstop.

Even though Jeff would land a Poetry in Motion on Edge and Matt would nail Christian with his Twist of Faith maneuver in the opening moments, the reigning champs had the early "edge" in the bout. Jeff was pushed down off the top of the cage by Edge, leaving Matt to battle the duo by himself for a while in the padlocked cage.

After Edge & Christian worked over a helpless Matt for a while, Jeff was able to confiscate the key to the cage's door, open it, and throw in a chair to try and help out his brother. This once again got the tagger involved in the action. The Hardy Boyz would eventually get the win by way of steel chairs as they both clobbered Edge simultaneously while he was trying to climb his way out of the ring.

Although they won the straps on this night, the action didn't compare to their match at WrestleMania 2000. The tag tandem wouldn't face only Edge & Christian on this memorable April night in Anaheim, California, they would also face off against the destructive Dudley Boyz in a Triple Ladder match.

This match had everything. Tables and ladders and chairs ... oh my! The Dudleyz were their

Pics Pix

typical table-smashing selves, while Edge & Christian were busy double-suplexing their foes. The Hardyz were their high-flying, acrobatic selves, sailing from the top of the ladders and ropes numerous times. Jeff would nail an awesome Swanton Bomb from the top of a ladder on Buh Buh Ray Dudley while Matt would hit a Twist of Fate on D-Von Dudley inside the ring. But the dueling brothers would go home on this night without the belt or the win as Edge & Christian would gain the victory.

The first three-way was so entertaining that the duos would do it again four months later at SummerSlam. The match was entitled the Tables, Ladders, and Chairs match and took place in Raleigh, North Carolina, in late August. The tag belts would not only be on the line on this night, they would actually be suspended from the arena ceiling over the ring and the first duo to come down with them would become the new champions.

The action was fast and furious as the six men would use everything in their arsenal to get the win. The Dudleyz again opted to put people through tables. Edge tried his luck with some chair shots and the Hardyz flew into action from atop the arena on the ladders. As a matter of fact, Jeff at one point was hanging from midair from one of the championship belts with D-Von on the other, but neither could hang on. The team that did hang on for the win that night was Edge & Christian.

Although they don't always come away with the W, The Hardy Boyz are by no means losers. The good-guy grapplers are risk takers in the squared circle and are well worth the price of admission. Still in their twenties, the dynamic duo will be entertaining the wrestling audience for many more years to come.

Bret Hart

Bret "The Hitman" Hart is a wrestler who truly has wrestling in his blood. Born in Calgary, Alberta, in July of 1957 to Stu and Helen Hart, this youngster followed in his dad's bootsteps and pursued a career in pro wrestling. He became a student of the game not only through watching his dad in the ring, but by also attending his father's wrestling school, The Dungeon, which was located in the basement of the Hart household. The Dungeon has produced many wrestling successes over the years, such as Chris Jericho, Chris Benoit, "Rowdy" Roddy Piper, Jim "The Anvil" Neidhart, and Davey

Howard Kernats

Boy Smith, but none can compare to Stu's star student, his son Bret.

"The Hitman" hit the amateur grappling circuits in his early teens, where he won city and provincial championships in three different weight classes and then would turn pro at the tender age of twenty-one, debuting against a wrestler by the name of Dennis Stamp. Having learned the tricks of the trade early on from his Hall-of-Fame father, Bret mastered the fundamentals of wrestling and would quickly move up the ladder of each federation he joined. He would make a name for himself in Canada as a champion in the Hart-promoted federation known as Stampede Wrestling. From there he would make stops in the AWA, NWA, and also on the Japanese and European circuits, honing his skills.

Then, in 1984, he received the call he had been waiting for all his life. The owner of the World Wrestling Federation, Vince McMahon, wanted the Calgary native to come join his federation as a babyface wrestler. Hart immediately took the WWF head honcho up on the offer, but he didn't remain a face for long as "The Hitman" was paired with his brother-in-law Jim "The Anvil" Neidhart, and the two of them would wreak havoc on the WWF as members of the Hart Foundation along with their manager Jimmy "The Mouth of the South" Hart.

Ironically, the Hart Foundation began a feud with the British Bulldogs, which was comprised of the Dynamite Kid and Davey Boy Smith, not only another graduate of the Dungeon training program, but also another Hart brother-in-law. Neidhart and Hart would capture their first tag title from the Bulldogs on January 26, 1987, in Tampa, Florida.

While Hart went on to win another tag title in his WWF tenure, all throughout his stay in the federation he had but one title on his mind—the world heavyweight championship. In stunning fashion, the technically sound and powerful wrestler copped the ultimate WWF prize an impressive five times during his thirteen-year WWF stay. "The Hitman" garnered his first heavyweight championship belt on October 12, 1992, as he defeated the "Nature Boy" Ric Flair in Canada. He would lose the strap to Yokozuna less than six months later, but would regain the title from the big grappler on March 20, 1994, in New York. Hart would hold the prestigious title three more times in his career, with the last coming on August 3, 1997, against The Undertaker.

Also throw in his two Intercontinental belt championships, his two King of the Ring titles, his Superstar of the Year honor in 1993, and you have one hell of a federation run. But 1997 would mark the end of his WWF association when he left for the greener pastures of WCW after a bitter falling out with McMahon at an event in front of his hometown Canadian fans.

The good guy wrestler went ballistic on the WWF owner when

McMahon turned the tables on him and changed the outcome of a match in Montreal on November 9, 1997, between Hart and Shawn Michaels, causing Hart to lose his title to "The Heartbreak Kid." Even though it was a known fact that Hart was leaving the WWF once his contract expired, he wasn't supposed to drop the belt until December, at least so he thought.

But McMahon had other plans, so when Michaels had "The Hitman" in his own sharpshooter hold, McMahon ordered the bell to be rung, declaring Michaels the victor. Immediately following the bell, Michaels dashed from the ring with a confused look on his face, not knowing what had just happened, but having sense enough to realize that "The Hitman" was not going to be happy about the outcome.

The unhappy camper first took his frustrations out on the TV monitors at ringside, and then he found the WWF boss and spit right in McMahon's face on his way back to the locker rooms to find and confront Michaels. When he found "The Heartbreak Kid," he questioned him as to what just went on out there, and Michaels claimed to not have known a thing about the bogus bell ringing himself.

Hart would then hunt down McMahon and live up to his Hitman nickname and pummel his boss, thus exiting the federation in a style that "Stone Cold" Steve Austin would be proud of.

Hart made his WCW debut at a Souled Out event, where he faced and defeated former WWFer Ric Flair, taking him out with one of his deadly sharpshooter moves. Hart was now on his way to another glorious title run. He would start off by garnering the U.S. belt four times and then gradually work his way to the top of the WCW mountain by winning the heavyweight championship title on November 21, 1999, against Chris Benoit in front of his family, friends, and fans in Toronto's Air Canada Centre. This win would put him in an elite class of five— Ric Flair, Randy Savage, Hulk Hogan, and Kevin Nash—the only wrestlers to ever have won the heavyweight titles in both the WWF and WCW in their careers.

This awesome grappler would also garner the tag-team championship strap as he teamed with another WCW powerhouse, Goldberg, to win the title on December 7, 1999. Later on in the month he would win his second WCW World Heavyweight title on December 20 in Baltimore, adding more gold to his wrestling legacy.

Throughout his career, Hart has at one time or another been the best and battled the best. Lately, his career has been slowed by severe injuries, and no one is quite certain where that leaves this legendary warrior. Only Hart knows for sure how much he has left in the tank, and only time will tell if he ever graces the ring again with his presence. But the one thing that is for certain when it comes to Hart, whether he wrestled as a heel or hero, he always gave his fans their money's worth.

Hulk Hogan

erry Bollea, a.k.a. Hulk Hogan, has proven to the wrestling world that he can not only thrive as both a heel and a hero, but more important, that he can take a floundering wrestling organization and raise it to heights never before reached. Hulk Hogan is without a doubt the singular, most important wrestler of all time. Bollea was able to cross wrestling over into the mainstream market on his showmanship alone.

Howard Kernats

Hogan was able not only to knock over his opponents in the ring, he was also able to help knock over some barriers that turned wrestling from a "sport" into sports-entertainment. He helped pioneer wrestling into a multimillion dollar industry that combines the competitiveness of wrestling with soap opera–like storylines.

But before Bollea would help transform the industry, he, like any other wrestler, had to pay his dues. The legendary Jack Brisco discovered him one night and talked him into giving the business a try. Bollea would also call on the services of Japanese legend Hiro Matsuda and begin a hard training regimen under the veteran matsman.

When he was ready to face the music, Bollea hit the independent circuits under the Sterling Golden moniker. The 6-foot-7, 275-pound wrestler would immediately find success and make a name for himself in his early years. Speaking of names, he would then change his ring name to Terry Boulder and began branching out and competing in larger wrestling regions such as the AWA and WWWF, as the WWF was then called. While carding in these promotions, he was being managed by "Classy" Freddie Blassie and also wrestling as a heel.

Though he was quickly turning heads and gaining quite a following, his popularity didn't skyrocket until he made an appearance in the motion picture *Rocky III* as the wrestling villain Thunderlips, alongside Sylvester Stallone and Mr. T. Wrestling genius Vince McMahon, Jr., took notice of Bollea's success from the movie and quickly moved to make him the focal point of his wrestling organization, the World Wrestling Federation.

Before you knew it, Bollea, now known as Hulk Hogan, was wrestling for the heavyweight championship title from the Iron Sheik, and when he won that prestigious belt on January 23, 1984, it was the start of the coming of age of modern-day wrestling. The main piece of the puzzle, Hogan, was in place.

The next stop for Hogan from here was the first "Super Bowl" of wrestling, WrestleMania. This event really put wrestling on the mainstream map. The extravaganza was held in the world's most famous arena, Madison Square Garden, and it would be the first time that the "sport" crossed paths with celebrities from all walks of life. Muhammad Ali was there as the guest referee. Mr. T was there to take part in a match with Hogan. Even rock star Cyndi Lauper was there taking in the action.

Hogan, who was now playing the role of WWF hero in more ways than one, had brought the industry front and center, and if he had failed to carry this event, wrestling very well may have crumbled and stayed as the low-key, high school gymnasium audience sport that it had been. But with a little help from his wrestling buddies, and mastermind Vince McMahon, Hogan would not disappoint. The main clash at 'Mania was a typical good guy/bad guy build-up between Hulk Hogan and his archenemy at the time, "Rowdy" Roddy Piper.

When all was said and done, Hulk Hogan and Mr. T defeated Roddy Piper and Paul Orndorff on March 31, 1985, in the main event at WrestleMania. Although this was a shining moment for wrestling and the WWF at the time, it was just the tip of the iceberg for Hogan. One of the main indicators that the event was successful and that it was well-received came a few weeks after the gala, when Hulk Hogan's face graced the cover of *Sports Illustrated*. The issue would go on to be the magazine's top-selling issue of the year, besides the annual swimsuit edition, of course.

But Hulk wasn't finished there.

It wasn't until WrestleMania III that Hogan really left his BIGGEST impression on the federation and his fans.

The WWF event was loaded with many outstanding matches and it had also broken all sorts of indoor sporting event records for attendance. WrestleMania III sold out the Pontiac Silverdome to the tune of 92,000 people. The main event was to have an even bigger impact than the crowd number, as one wrestling giant would face another. Hulk Hogan would face off that night against grappling great Andre the Giant, and would not only beat the undefeated legend, but even more impressively, would lift the 7-foot, 500-pound monster over his head and slam him to the canvas, bringing down the house.

This was the type of match that would go down in history and last a lifetime. If you were present in Michigan that night, you certainly will remember the thud of Andre hitting the mat. Even if you were at home watching, you still vividly remember the slam.

For the next ten years, Hogan would entertain his WWF fans, and then, when the federation started to change gears and go in a new direction with the younger stars, Hogan moved on. He would take some time off from the ring to pursue his acting career. Then Ted Turner came calling with an offer and a challenge, and Hulk was not one to turn down either.

Hogan, now known as "Hollywood," signed on to World Championship Wrestling, where he again was asked to help bring a drowning wrestling organization into prominence. Surprisingly enough, Hogan brought the WCW into the limelight when he teamed with Kevin Nash and Scott Hall (two ex-WWFers) to form the New World Order, a clique that loved wreaking havoc on the federation. Even though this role was new and different from the one he had played for so many years in the WWF, it didn't stop him from being successful. Gone were the days of him wearing his infamous yellow and red outfit and preaching to his little Hulkamaniacs to say their prayers and take their vitamins. He now donned the black and white of the nWo and was ready to be a badass heel for his new league.

"Hollywood" Hogan would then jump back and forth from the heel to hero persona at WCW, but history has proven that no matter the federation or wrestling personality, Hulk Hogan will go down as a wrestler who was strong enough to carry two federations on his broad shoulders. More important, he will go down as one of the all-time greats.

Jeff Jarrett

To say that Jeff Jarrett is a proven winner would be an understatement. Before the Nashville native had even one wrestling-boot fitted leg onto a mat in the big two, he had already been a champion twenty-five times over when he'd fought in the smaller wrestling federations, the USWA and the CWA.

Jarrett can thank his dad, Jerry Jarrett, for introducing him to the business. His father was a promoter for a local Memphis wrestling federation. But even before the young Jarrett would make his grappling debut as a wrestler, he had already tried his hand at refereeing the rough and tumble sport.

Soon enough, he had turned in his black-and-white striped shirt for a pair of wrestling trunks and boots. He would make his pro debut for his dad's Memphis promotion in April 1986 and wouldn't disappoint his father, defeating his opponent, Tony Falk, in stunning fashion. It was all uphill for the young wrestler from there as he marched his way through the small federations, piling up the wins along the way.

These wins didn't come against just any slouches, either. Along the way, Jarrett tussled with Jerry Lawler several times, one match coming on October 6, 1990, for the USWA Southern title, which Jarrett won. The Tennessee titan even met face-to-face with the vicious Moondogs, as he teamed with Robert Fuller against the dominant duo. There were even memorable clashes with Lex Luger and Brian Christopher early on in Jarrett's career.

Then in 1994, Jarrett got the call for the big time. The WWF wanted his services and the Music City native was there in a heartbeat.

Although he would make his debut in 1994 as Double J, Jarrett wouldn't make many friends.

He showed promise early on in his matches, but his act of billing himself as the greatest country singer that ever lived was starting to wear thin with his fellow grapplers. They even exposed the wrestler to the audience as a "fraud" who was lip-synching his hit song!

But all these distractions probably stemmed from their being jealous of Jarrett's success since he'd won the Intercontinental title in no time upon entering the federation. On January 22, 1995, Jarrett won the IC belt from Razor Ramon at Royal Rumble in Tampa, Florida.

The IC belt would go back and forth over the next six months, with Jarrett taking in another two titles before he lost the strap to "The Heartbreak Kid" Shawn Michaels on July 23, 1995. Michaels did break Jarrett's heart on this night as the grappler not only took his title away that night, he more embarrassingly beat Jarrett in front of his hometown fans in Nashville.

Not too pleased with what had happened on that night, Jarrett took some time off from the federation and returned briefly, but eventually wound up with World Championship Wrestling where, in November 1996, he immediately began stirring the pot. He would have run-ins with all of the federation's top talent in his first go-around with the WCW. Top dogs like Hulk Hogan, Ric Flair, The Giant, Sting, Arn Anderson, Chris Benoit, and Steve McMichael, all at one time or another wanted a piece of Jarrett.

The pesky wrestler even managed to garner some gold during his first run with the WCW. Jarrett would win the U.S. title belt from Dean Malenko on June 9, 1997, in Boston, Massachusetts, with a little help from Eddie Guerrero.

His contract with the WCW would expire that October, and when negotiations on a new deal broke down, Jarrett returned to the WWF with his old persona, Double J, but a new nasty attitude. Double J now loved to make sweet music by bashing guitars over his opponents' heads. In his time back with the federation, the colorful and talented grappler wouldn't just make some noise, he would also come away with some gold.

In his second go-around with the WWF, Jarrett won four more Intercontinental belts, one tag-team title, and the European strap. The tag-team title was the first of the golden belts he would wear during his second stint with the federation.

Jarrett would team up with Owen Hart on January 25, 1999, against Ken Shamrock and the Big Boss Man, and together they would dethrone the tag champs. He would then win the fourth IC belt of his career on May 25, 1999, when he met up with and defeated The Godfather in Moline, Illinois.

Double J would not only garner two more IC belts in the next three months, he would also add the European title to his resume. On August 22, 1999, at SummerSlam, he defeated D'Lo Brown in Minneapolis, Minnesota, to become the new Euro champ.

But Jarrett started to take his bashing to another level as he began attacking the women of the federation, saying that they should be barefoot, pregnant, and home in the kitchen making dinner instead of out making a name and a living for themselves.

Well, Chyna didn't take a liking to those words and went on to beat the woman-basher in a match entitled Good Housekeeping on October 17, 1999, at a No Mercy event in Cleveland, Ohio. Even more impressive was that she went home that night with his IC belt draped over her shoulder.

The next night, the guitar-swinging heel would bolt to the WCW for a second go-around and he would make a smashing entrance by belting Buff Bagwell over the noggin with his musical weapon. Upon reentering the federation, he dubbed himself The Chosen One.

Within one year, the full-of-himself wrestler won the U.S. title, the second of his career, over Chris Benoit on December 20, 1999. He would win his third U.S. belt a little less than a month later on January 17, 2000.

But the best was yet to come for the kabonging grappler. Three months later at Spring Stampede, Jarrett would win his first WCW World Heavyweight title as he beat Diamond Dallas Page with a little help from DDP's beautiful wife, Kimberly.

Jarrett would lose the belt to Page a couple of weeks later in a controversial tag-team match involving actor David Arquette, but The Chosen One would go on to win the world strap two more times in the next month in what was an interesting sequence of events.

While his mouth is one of his greatest weapons—known for calling opponents "slapnuts" and "slappy"—his in-ring skills are second to none. Jarrett is blessed with great technical skills and uses a finishing move that's an inverted Russian leg sweep called "The Stroke." And according to his official WCW bio, his wrestling style can best be described as a little bit of country and a little bit of smash and roll.

And if all else fails, The Chosen One will just resort to his trusty guitar for help!

Chris Jericho

On August 9, 1999, the World Wrestling Federation welcomed one of sports-entertainment's future superstars, Chris Jericho. The 6-foot, 231-pound grappler made his federation debut in memorable fashion as he not only appeared live on a RAW IS WAR card from Chicago, but came out while The Rock was doing an interview and interrupted the WWF's number one superstar.

Also, at the time of his entrance, the federation was making

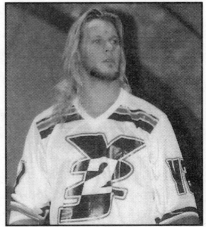

Howard Kernats

a fuss about the coming of the new millennium and had had a countdown clock in place for weeks which was supposedly running down the days until the year 2000, or, more specifically, the dawning of a new era. Little did anyone know that it had nothing to do with the year 2000. The countdown was all about the new age of wrestling and the WWF officials sent a message loud and clear as to who they felt was going to carry the federation into the new era—"The Lionheart" Chris Jericho.

The millennium clock wound down to zero upon his arrival and Jericho immediately stole the show by claiming the program to be his, stating to the crowd: "Welcome to WAR IS JERICHO!" Not only did Jericho debut by interrupting The Rock, he also came into the arena in half-time show–like fashion, with loud rock music blaring throughout the facility and fireworks covering the ceiling. It was truly an awesome display for someone who hadn't even seen any ring action in the federation.

He would get into a match that night, but it wasn't physical—purely vocal. It would still send a message to all who were watching and listening. Jericho wouldn't get a piece of The Rock that night, but he certainly would give him a piece of his mind. The WWF's new arrival claimed that he was there to not only save the crowd from The People's Champion's boring interview, but more important, he was there to carry the federation on his back as he was now the new WWF party host.

Well, this didn't go over too well with The Rock, and he would later become more enraged as Jericho interfered in his match against The Big Show. His interference didn't affect the outcome of The Rock's match, as he still got the win, but the fact that Jericho was interfering in one of his matches didn't sit well with the popular wrestler.

Speaking of popular, that's just what Jericho was becoming with the fans. He was enjoying the push being given to him by the federation higher-ups, and although he hasn't surpassed The Rock as the WWF's No. 1 babyface, he's well on his way to superstardom.

But Jericho hadn't always wrestled as a face during his career. As a matter of fact, his biggest popularity run in World Championship Wrestling came when he was a crybaby heel. Jericho had arrived in the WCW about the same time that many former WWF stars had come onboard, and his character was basically playing second fiddle to these guys. He was involved with storylines that weren't getting him noticed, so the wrestler decided to take matters into his own hands—fists, in this case.

One night, after an unexpected loss in the ring, he took out his frustrations by cursing, pounding his fists and breaking everything in sight. The following week, he would apologize to the wrestling audience for his actions and would promise to never throw a tantrum like that again. But Jericho would break this promise night after night by throwing tantrum after tantrum. This would not only fuel his fire in the ring, it would also put him over with the fans. Though they booed the tantrum-throwing villain, it didn't matter, as he was drawing a response from the WCW fans like never before.

Despite these actions being out of character for the high-flying, acrobatic wrestler, it didn't phase him one bit. All he wanted was to fit in and be noticed, and he learned the hard way that nice guys sometimes need to kick it up a notch in order to get attention and respect.

"I remember the old sportswriter of years ago who said, 'In professional contact sports, nice guys finish last.' Well, I learned that eventually, though it took me awhile," he explained. "I've been around and abused by some of the big names of the WCW, and I was getting a little tired of being abused. So I changed my ways and decided to create a different attitude. If that's how I want to wrestle, then I have that right."

Jericho was at a point in his career that he wanted to be wrestling with the big boys; after all, that was the federation's motto, and he wanted to be a part of the big-time action. He knew he was being paid a great sum of money to grapple on this level, and he wanted to give the organization and fans their money's worth, even if it meant stepping on some toes and hearing boos from the crowd.

"A lot of fans don't like me. They boo me and carry these big insulting signs at the arenas, but it doesn't bother me," he claimed at the time. "I'm making big bucks and climbing to the top and that's what's important." In a short amount of time Jericho had won six different titles in the WCW, but he wanted more. He knew he had what it took to be heavyweight champ, and he wanted his fair shot.

"Just like WCW says—'where the big boys play'—and that's who I want to fight with," a frustrated Jericho said. "Not these chumps with no size or strength. I like tough competition. I'm not afraid of it, and I'm always eager to take on any and all challengers. That's why Chris Jericho has gone so far in wrestling, 'cause I'm ready for anything."

The WCW bad guy wanted a piece of the federation's top good guy, who also happened to be the WCW's No. 1 star, Goldberg. But the top officials weren't buying what he was selling.

This would be the beginning of the end of his WCW career and he would move on to more challenging pastures at the WWF. Here he would also thrive in no time. From his first entrance up until today, Jericho has been all and more of what he was advertised to be. Although he admitted to being nervous on his opening night, he was more than ready.

"I'm not going to lie and say I wasn't nervous," he said, "but I was nervous in a way that I knew it was my time to shine. This was it, my time had finally come, and I deserved it. Not because I'm some kind of extraordinary talent or anything, but because I've been working my butt off for nine years to get there and I was ready for it. It was a huge entrance and a huge amount of hype, but I knew I could live up to it and people wouldn't be disappointed. I don't think I've disappointed so far."

Jericho is certainly right about that. The Ayatollah of Rock 'n Roll-a has more than lived up to the hype. He has surely stood up to and been involved with many of the federation's biggest stars in his short time there. As a matter of fact, the week after he made his debut, he stepped into the ring with literally two of the WWF's biggest stars in The Big Show and The Undertaker. The two towering grapplers were doing an interview on RAW IS WAR, and Jericho decided it was his duty to save the fans yet again from another boring segment. Even though The Undertaker was less than thrilled by his presence, the fans were hyped as he was proving little by little that he didn't care who was in the ring. He was ready to face any and all "takers."

Another wrestler who was less than thrilled by his presence was Triple H. The WWF's baddest heel got into a feud with the baby-faced Jericho for some time because Jericho began trash talking his wife, Stephanie McMahon-Helmsley. These words would cause a classic clash of good against bad.

At one time or another Jericho has gone at it with The Road Dogg, Chyna, The Rock, Chris Benoit, Ken Shamrock, Kurt Angle, Jeff Hardy, Eddie Guerrero, and many more. The list just keeps getting bigger and bigger, just like the wrestler himself. There's no limit to Jericho's potential, and who knows how long he'll stay a face, but you can bet your bottom dollar that he'll wear heavyweight gold in the near future.

Kane

Believe it or not, Kane has played both a heel and a face in his time wrestling for the World Wrestling Federation. But with his enormous size, physique, costume, and gimmick, he is far better suited to his demonic role.

The 7-foot grappler, who is the long-lost brother of The Undertaker, stormed onto the WWF scene on Monday, October 5, 1997, when he made a surprise appearance during one of his brother's matches at an event entitled Badd Blood. Kane would help his brother's opponent, Shawn "Boy Toy" Michaels, escape the Hell in a Cell match with

Howard Kernats

a victory that night as the monstrous wrestler tore off the door of the cage to get to his brother.

Once Kane was inside the cell, he took it upon himself to confront and choke slam his confused and surprised brother. This violent act would not only stun the crowd and the 'Taker, it would also allow Michaels to get the pin and win as he had been getting manhandled by the dark warrior from pillar to post before Kane interfered in the contest.

This would be only the start of Kane's havoc-wreaking on the federation. Under the guidance of Paul Bearer, The Undertaker's former mentor, Kane would interfere in numerous matches on RAW IS WAR broadcasts, causing chaos throughout the entire WWF.

One of his attack victims was Dude Love, who experienced Kane's wrath and choke slam firsthand on RAW. As a result the grappler was knocked out of action. This would set up Kane's first real match in the federation against Mankind, who was slated to go to war against the out-of-control wrestler to try and get revenge on the Big Red Machine for taking out his alter ego, Love.

But the battle of the masked warriors would not wind up in Mankind's favor. Kane defeated the grappler courtesy of his treacherous tombstone pile driver. Many were trying and many were failing in their efforts to stop the seemingly unstoppable creature. Kane seemed to be able to do whatever he wanted, wherever he wanted, to whomever he wanted.

But his rage was aimed mostly at his "brother," who supposedly had set their house on fire, "killing" their "parents" and him in the process. Obviously, Kane had survived and the only question that remained to be answered was how far would he go in order to get back at his brother?

Kane would again interfere that year in one of his brother's matches. This time The Undertaker was squaring off against Jeff Jarrett. Although Kane's interference didn't allow his brother to lose this time, it actually helped him win, he still managed to brutally attack his sibling afterward. But The Undertaker stated that he would not fight his own flesh and blood.

The sick and sadistic would occur at the 1998 Royal Rumble main event match, where The Undertaker would again square off against Shawn Michaels. During the contest, which was labeled a casket match, many wrestlers came from backstage to try and help Michaels get the win over his towering opponent, but none were successful. Finally, when The Undertaker had become totally outnumbered in the ring, his brother Kane came to the rescue. Or did he?

Once the ring was cleared of the attackers, Kane went on the offensive and began laying the smack down again on his surprised brother, stuffing him in the casket. Enter Paul Bearer, who helped The Big Red Machine lock his brother into the death box, rolling it away from the squared circle. The two maniacs then stopped in front of the wrestler's entrance, and Kane climbed on top of the casket, ax in hand, and began chopping away. While he sliced and diced, Bearer got hold of some gasoline and matches and handed them over to his monster.

Kane then doused the casket in the ignitable fluid and proceeded to get revenge on The Undertaker by sending him back to his maker in hell. Or did he?

Right before WrestleMania XIV, The Undertaker would reappear on RAW IS WAR, setting up a grudge match between the two brothers. The Undertaker was now ready and willing to take on his own flesh and blood.

The 'Taker would get revenge on his bro at 'Mania, who tombstoned him twice to no avail, as The Undertaker took him out with a lethal pile driver for the win.

The two siblings would do battle many times over after this, including an inferno match where The Undertaker won by setting his brother ablaze. But while Kane loved battling with his brother, he also wanted to take home some gold.

He would win the federation's most coveted belt, the World Heavyweight Championship title—even though his reign lasted only twenty-four hours—in a match on June 28, 1998, at the King of the Ring tournament against "Stone Cold" Steve Austin in Pittsburgh, Pennsylvania. The Big Red Machine has also been a tag-team belt winner three times in his career.

Kane would also turn corporate for a while, being at one time the main bodyguard for Vince McMahon. While he was one of McMahon's best back-watchers ever, he was still more valuable and effective as a prime-time player between the ropes.

The guess here is that Kane will become an even bigger monster in the ring and will be a top contender for the title for a long time to come, and once he gets it, watch out, because his reign will no doubt last longer than twenty-four hours next time around.

Kidman

Howard Kernats

Billy Kidman is a World Wrestling Federation fan favorite, especially with women. His movie star looks and wrestling arsenal is what makes this 5-foot-11, 195-pound grappler stick out in the wrestling crowd.

Kidman was overlooked early on in his career strictly because of his size. Promoters took one look at him and questioned as to how he would make it in a business where only the rough, tough, and massive survive. But the WCW young gun proved them all wrong, possessing a style that combines Luchador maneuvers with some classic mat moves. He also has a threshold for pain that is second to none in the business. And he needs it with the amount of punishment he endures against his bigger foes.

What makes him so successful against these larger-than-life opponents is his quickness and versatility in the ring. Another impressive weapon he possesses is the ability to execute the lethal Shooting Star Press, a dazzling move made famous by Jushin "Thunder" Liger.

Kidman worked his way up the wrestling ranks by battling in many indy federations, one being the ECW, before landing in the WCW. He came onboard and immediately proved that, pound-for-pound, he was one of the federation's best wrestlers. He debuted as part of Raven's Flock and has been known to latch on with wrecking groups every now and again. Another one of these cliques was the Filthy Animals, where he was a member with Konnan and Rey Mysterio, Jr.

The Pennsylvania native would capture the cruiserweight title and tag strap (with Konnan) within no time, making the other grapplers aware of what he could do in the ring in spite of his size. Heel or hero, Kidman has what it takes to succeed in the biz. The WCW needs to focus more on "kids" like him in order to be able to compete with the big boys.

Konnan

Howard Kernats

The World Wrestling Federation has the Road Dogg and World Championship Wrestling has its very own canine in K-Dogg; better known as Konnan.

This 5-foot-10, 250-pound grappler is a unique combination of size, strength, and high-flying maneuvers, which stems from his lucha libre background. Also unique to this wrestler is the route he took to get to the big time. Konnan has always had a love for the ring, but it hasn't always been the wrestling ring. This Mexico City native loved boxing and was a member of the U.S. Navy boxing team, where he learned how to use his hands as deadly weapons.

This experience led him to the squared circle in Mexico, where he became an instant superstar in the AA Lucha Libre league. Early on he would not only wrestle with a mask, but he also went by the moniker of Konnan El Barbaro. As he developed, he would drop the mask and barbarian title from his ring name and make a new name for himself simply as Konnan.

In 1996, he came to the WCW from the ECW and won the U.S. strap at Superbrawl from One Man Gang, proving that on this night "One Man" was not enough to hold this fiery wrestler down. Konnan would also hook up with several factions. At one time or another he could be found hanging with the New World Order, The Dungeon of Doom, the Filthy Animals or nWo Wolfpac. He was also a member of a heel group known as Los Gringos Locos. This clique included Eddie Guerrero, Art Barr, and Louie Spicolli.

Konnan is a new-age wrestler who not only can talk a good game, but who can also beat his opponent in several different ways. If his high-flying moves aren't cutting it one night, he has the ability to take out his foe with some brute strength and force. This is one stray Dogg that grapplers don't want to mess with.

Shane McMahon

I'm sure it's not easy being Shane McMahon, the boss's son, but it sure must be a lot of fun! Shane O' Mac has not only proven himself able to wrestle and take bumps with the best of 'em the last couple of years, he has also been able to do his part on the business end as well, helping to keep the World Wrestling Federation running like a well-oiled machine.

Shane, like his dad, Vince, knows what the people want and don't want to see in the grappling game. They both realize that professional wrestling is no longer a sport, but sports-entertainment. And they aim to please, even if it means sacrificing their own bodies for the good of the federation.

"Shane knows his role," Vince said in an interview with *TV Guide*. "He's here to get wrestlers over [with the crowd], to get other performers over."

And Shane has done just that ever since he first came onto the wrestling scene. One of the first instances when the crowd took to Shane came in March 1999. The younger McMahon was trying to get over as a rich, snobby heel with the crowd and in order to do this he'd brought along two of his real childhood friends, Pete Gas and Rodney to help him.

Rodney and Gas helped their childhood buddy make the scenario in a Greenwich Street Fight against X-Pac on a RAW IS WAR broadcast so believable that before you knew it, the trio had made their way to WrestleMania XV to continue the saga.

While Gas and Rodney needed to be given some of the credit, most of it belonged to Shane. He could have taken the easy way out and gone with pros to help him "get over," but like his dad, he doesn't like the easy way. He likes to do things his way.

The thirty-year-old heat generator has found success on his own in the WWF and has also been aligned with some of the most interesting characters in sports-entertainment today. At one time or another, Shane has been linked with The Undertaker and The Corporate Ministry, Edge & Christian, Chris Benoit, The Big Show, Test, The McMahon-Helmsley faction, and The Corporation.

He has also garnered the Hardcore Championship and the European title in his short time between the ropes. But in-ring accomplishments aside, the most impressive achievement to date for this young WWF honcho is that he has proven without a shadow of a doubt to his dad and the wrestling fans alike that the future of the WWF is safe in his hands.

Vince McMahon, Jr.

There's only one word that can describe Vince McMahon, Jr., these days, and it's not heel or hero. It's "genius."

The modern-day P. T. Barnum bought a wrestling organization, the Capitol Wrestling Corporation, from his father, Vince McMahon, Sr., in the early eighties and turned it into the multimillion dollar company that today is the World Wrestling Federation. The young McMahon had the foresight to change the image of wrestling from "sport" to sports-entertainment. He wanted to maximize the abilities of his ring stars by having them perform both in and out of the ring.

And McMahon didn't limit his breeding grounds to just the weight lifters. The full-time grapplers were no longer the typical musclebound gym rats. They were being plucked off pro and college football fields, basketball courts, off Olympic mats, boxing rings, and even Hollywood movie sets. McMahon didn't care about their backgrounds, just whether or not they could sell his product to his target audience.

The North Carolina native was as shrewd as he was smart. He sold people on his wares, and they came along for the ride. And what a ride it has been! The WWF head honcho persuaded celebrities such as Cyndi Lauper, Muhammad Ali, Mr. T, Pete Rose, Lawrence Taylor, Mike Tyson, and countless others to take part at one time or another in one of his shows.

The start of his reign as wrestling's ring king came in 1984, when he signed on Hulk Hogan to take his federation in this new direction. The Hulkster was becoming a media monster after his appearance in *Rocky III* as the surly villain Thunderlips, who wrestled Rocky Balboa in an exhibition match in the movie. The audience was fixed on the grappler who threw Rocky out of the ring in the famous flick, so Mc-Mahon went out and hired Hogan.

While McMahon knew Hogan wasn't the greatest technical wrestler in the business, he saw something in the monstrous matsman that no one had seen before. Hogan was a showman first and a wrestler second, and this was exactly what McMahon was looking for. He wanted to transform the industry into a competitive event that had soap opera–like storylines.

He knew that this went against everything that his dad and grand-father, who were pioneers in the wrestling industry way before Jr. had gotten involved, believed in. Yet, he, along with Hogan, still leaned in this direction and made wrestling what it is today.

Almost immediately McMahon, who was also doubling as the federation ring announcer, made his meal ticket, Hogan, win the championship title from the Iron Sheik. He knew the two had bigger fish to fry if they were going to take wrestling in a new direction. His next step was to create storylines that not only kept the fans interested, but ones that would make them salivate for more on a weekly basis.

One of the main angles was the good guy/bad guy feud between Hulk Hogan and "Rowdy" Roddy Piper. McMahon knew that in order to have a hero, he also needed a heel who was not only believable, but one whom the audience would love to hate. And Piper would play this role perfectly.

The back and forth action of good vs. evil led the audience and federation to the next plateau. The wrestling mastermind would now take his storyline and show one step further by putting together the "Super Bowl" of wrestling, WrestleMania, and holding it in a place for the whole world to see: the world's most famous arena, Madison Square Garden.

McMahon would put his money, ass, and neck out on the limb for this extravaganza, counting on the fans to not only buy into the concept, but more important, buy tickets! The WWF boss figured that if he was going to do it, he may as well do it right. If he failed, he failed *big*. But that's what makes him so successful. That's why he's one of a kind. If he's going to take chances, he goes all out. He leaves nothing out on the field (or mat in this case). He walks the walk and that's why he's able to talk the talk.

Well, we all know the outcome. WrestleMania was a huge success, and still is to this day, and though Hulkamania was running wild in the eighties, McMahon wasn't done yet. He had achieved his goal of taking wrestling from the regional markets to a national level, but he also knew he wasn't in this for the short term, he was in it for the long haul. So when his federation lost some of its luster and novelty for a while, he didn't panic. He just went home and thought it out and devised a new scheme. McMahon knew that the WWF needed to go in another direction—let's just say he thought his organization needed an "attitude" adjustment.

One of the casualties of this adjustment was the eighties cash cow Hogan, who jumped ship to the WCW, but McMahon was not worried because his eye for wrestling talent was second to none. The next superstar to step up to the plate for McMahon was "Stone Cold" Steve Austin.

Austin became as popular in the nineties as Hogan had been in the eighties and "Stone Cold" has McMahon for thank for that. The WWF honcho literally helped make Austin into the most beloved grappler in the business as he wrote himself into the scripts and played the part of the heel boss who was trying to tell his employee what to do. Well, we all know that nobody can tell wrestling's meanest S.O.B. what to do, and consequently McMahon generated heat in the federation comparable, if not better than, the Rock-N-Wrestling days of the 1980s.

Vince basically figured that most people didn't like their boss and that this angle could bring a pretty good pop from his audience, so again he put his ass on the line. And once again he was right. Night after night fans were tuning in to see what was going to happen next between the disgruntled worker and the evil boss. Another impressive thing about the whole scenario was that McMahon knew that in order for this angle to go over and be believable, he would have to at some point get into a physical confrontation with Austin. Don't get me wrong, Vince is in great shape, but it's one thing to be in shape and another thing to take on a pro wrestler. But for the good of the company and audience he did it, and Austin roughed him up on several occasions.

Everyone loved the Austin/McMahon feud, especially the target audience, which was males 18–35 who could relate to the hated-boss angle. McMahon was giving his audience what they wanted. He would also start to include storylines that revolved around sex and violence. This would be a complete three-sixty from the Hogan days of milk, prayers, and vitamins, but McMahon again was not about image, he was about success and giving the audience what they wanted.

The nineties called for sex and violence, and McMahon went with the flow. He would now also bring into the mix his son, Shane, and daughter, Stephanie. Together the family took wrestling through the roof. For a while Vince went back to being a babyface character, but then would drop out of the picture for a while to give his kids some of the glory. McMahon would see his son's character, Shane, catch on with the audience as both a face and a heel and would even write his daughter into a scripted marriage with the WWF's most popular and hated heel ever, Triple H.

Howard Kernats

All in all, Vince McMahon, Jr., has been on a successful journey for over twenty years and has made an impact on the industry like none before him. Heel or hero, he has proven to be one of the country's savviest businessmen. According to an article published in the February 7, 2000, issue of *Newsweek*, McMahon has produced an empire that had projected sales of three hundred and forty million dollars for the year 2000, up two hundred and fifty million dollars from the previous season. The stock market values the WWF company to be worth an estimated one billion dollars.

While he may not be the best wrestler, ring announcer, or boss the WWF has ever had, he surely is one of the most important pioneers in the history of wrestling, and just what the doctor ordered for the federation.

Kevin Nash

If there was ever a wrestler who does what he wants when he wants, it's Kevin Nash. The 7-foot grappler made his pro debut in 1990 in the NWA and has kept on going.

He broke into the business first as a bodyguard for a female wrestler, Woman, but when the situation didn't work out for him outside the ring he took up the federation on an offer to work inside the ropes.

Nash joined the NWA as one half of a tag team called The Master Blasters as a personality called Steele. Although the duo patterned themselves after The Road Warriors, their partnership was

Howard Kernats

soon broken up. Nash would try two more personalities, Oz and Vinnie Vegas, in his stint with the NWA (which later became the WCW), but his characters just weren't going over with the crowd.

Not one to give up, the young wrestler turned to the WWF and Vince McMahon for help with his career. He would start out in the WWF just like he had in the WCW, as a bodyguard for a wrestler. But this time the results were different. Nash watched the back of one of the federation's all-time greats, Shawn "The Heartbreak Kid" Michaels.

The giant-sized wrestler's association with this great grappler would lead to bigger and better things for Nash. The new WWFer, now known as Diesel, was given a vote of confidence by McMahon when the federation owner pitted him against some of the organization's top talent and the 370-pound wrestler would not disappoint his new boss.

Diesel would win the Triple Crown of wrestling before his first year was completed in the WWF. He would hold the Intercontinental belt (beating Razor Ramon), the Tag Team belt (with Shawn Michaels), and the World Heavyweight championship (against Bob Backlund) all within months of one another. Of the three, the wrestler still holds his first WWF World title, nearest and dearest to his heart.

On November 26, 1994, Diesel would beat the legendary Backlund in front of a jam-packed audience in the world's most famous arena, Madison Square Garden. The fact that he won this match over an all-time great was impressive. The fact that he won the world title after being in the WWF for just under a year was also incredible, but the most amazing thing about this match was the way Nash won it. The Michigan native defeated his Hall-of-Fame opponent on that memorable November night in a measly eight seconds! If you were there and you blinked, you unfortunately would have missed it!

Then after several up and down years in the federation that saw him clash with both the WWF officials and some of the organization's talent, the tall, powerful entertainer decided it was time for a change and jumped ship after his contract expired. He, along with his partner in crime, Scott Hall, landed in the WCW in 1996.

Never one to pay any attention to authority, Nash decided to immediately rock the boat in his new federation. Along with Hall, the duo, now known as The Outsiders, decided they wanted to overthrow the entire wrestling organization and formed a rebel faction known as the New World Order, which not only became successful, but also carried the federation to heights and popularity way beyond imagination. Nash showed how much his stock had risen in the wrestling ranks when he convinced all-time good guy Hulk Hogan to turn in his red-and-yellow trunks for the bad black-and-white colors of the nWo.

One of his memorable rebel acts came on June 16, 1996, when he attacked his new boss, Eric Bischoff, at the Great American Bash at the Beach. Nash would show no mercy on this night as he powerbombed Bischoff through an interview table, proving that he would take on anyone to get control of the organization.

Over the years, this talented grappler has found success both on the tag circuit and in the singles ranks. While with WCW, the former college basketball star at the University of Tennessee has won five world championships and four tag-team titles. One of his high points in his WCW career came in December 1998, when he stopped Goldberg's unbeaten streak. The WCW rookie had come into the federation and piled up 173 wins until Nash got ahold of him on December 27 in Washington, DC, and brought him back down to earth.

Another reason Nash's success is an amazing story is that he never planned to be a pro grappler. He fell into the business when his professional basketball career went south because of a serious knee injury. He had parlayed a successful college hoops career, where he once had led the Vols to a Sweet 16 appearance in the Division I NCAA basketball tournament, into a chance to play pro basketball overseas in Germany. Nash took advantage of the opportunity and played in Europe for four years until his injury forced him to return to the States in 1990.

Although he has played both face and heel in his career, Nash seems better suited for the bad guy role. His size, brutality, and charisma always make him a force to be reckoned with. In 1997 Paul Wight, then known as The Giant (today known as The Big Show in the WWF), found this out the hard way when the two gargantua met in the ring and Big Sexy powerbombed his 500-pound foe into the mat and into the hospital. This awesome display of power caused the WCW to ban Nash from using this maneuver, citing that it was too dangerous to be used in the ring.

When asked about which role, babyface or heel, he prefers playing, he said that it didn't matter to him, as long as he and the audience are having a good time.

Rey Mysterio, Jr.

Rey Mysterio, Jr., is living proof that size doesn't matter. The 5-foot-3, 140-pound grappler has taken the WCW by storm winning five cruiserweight titles and two WCW tag belts so far in his career.

Mysterio began wrestling professionally at the tender age of sixteen, making his pro debut in 1990, in the sunny state of California, while still in high school. In order to get ready for his first pro match, against a wrestler named Shamu, he trained long and hard with his uncle, Rey Mysterio, Sr., the senior Rey taught him the ins and outs of the lucha libre style of wrestling, which from the age of fifteen he still uses to this day.

Howard Kernats

The young wrestler, who grew up in San Diego idolizing Ricky Steamboat, knew from early on what he wanted to do with his life, and before he had even graduated high school, he had put in two years on the pro circuit.

When he first broke into the wrestling world in the AAA and the WWA, he was known as Colibri, which is Spanish for *hummingbird*, and then sometime later he changed to the Super Nino moniker. But no matter the name, the results were always the same. The California native was a fan favorite who wrestled to please his audience, and who also had great success between the ropes. As a matter of fact, before he came to World Championship Wrestling, he had already won championship titles in the singles ranks. He garnered the WWA Cruiserweight title on three separate occasions, the WWA Welterweight belt two times, and the WWA World Light Heavyweight strap three different times.

The young lucha libre wrestler would also find success waiting for him in other wrestling ranks. On the tag circuit, he and his mentor, Uncle Rey, won a WWA Tag title. In the Mexican National Trios Championship, Rey, Jr., would team up with Octagon and Super Muneco and win the event.

There just seemed to be nothing this little guy couldn't accomplish in the ring.

Mysterio appeared on the national WCW scene as a masked warrior at a When Worlds Collide Pay-Per-View and was at first regarded as a novelty rather than a serious contender in the federation. But when upper management saw his acrobatic performances in the ring, they became hooked just as much as the audience and viewers did.

Mysterio wrestles with a style that showcases his blinding speed and aerial maneuvers, making him hard to beat because his opponents usually can't keep up with him or find him on the mat. As a matter of fact, they won't find him on the mat because half the time he's usually in the air zeroing in on his dizzy foe. His arsenal includes several high-risk moves, one being his lethal Huracanrana, which usually leaves the audience in awe.

Although Mysterio is regarded as the "King of Cruiserweights," he doesn't let his attributes stop him from taking on other wrestlers in bigger weight classes. The high-flying grappler recently shocked the fans and federation by squaring off and beating some of the biggest names and wrestlers in the business. He took on and beat Bam Bam Bigelow, the 6-foot-3, 325-pound, bald behemoth who is known for being a monster on the mat. Even more impressive was his victory over Kevin Nash, who stands at 7 foot, 356 pounds, and also is a nine-time WCW champion both on the singles and tag circuits. After pulling off these upsets, the tiny grappler made a name for himself in a big way and was dubbed "The Giant Killer."

Although he has found some success in factions and tag teams, Mysterio is a wrestler who works best alone. He also is one of the rare wrestlers who is popular with both fans and colleagues. This is both good and bad for the talented performer, as his game seems to suffer from his having too many friends in the ring. He needs to try and separate his associations with his coworkers when he steps between the ropes and concentrate on his opponent, because when he is focused, pound-for-pound, there's none better than Rey Mysterio, Jr.

Right to Censor

Right to Censor is a group of so-called concerned wrestlers who have taken it upon themselves to clean up the act of the World Wrestling Federation. Led by Steven Richards, who appointed himself the WWF censor, the posse has every intention of ridding the federation of any and all lewd, crude, and perverted acts.

Richards has recruited some of the federation's past sinners to help him fight his cause. Two of his soldiers, The Goodfather and Val Venis, were big-time "sinners" in the WWF at one time, but Richards has shown them the error of their ways and has placed them on a path to "righteousness."

The Goodfather, once known as The Godfather, used to parade around the ring in outlandish costumes, smoking big fat cigars, accompanied by his "Ho Train," a group of scantily clad women. But now he has left all that pimp and circumstance behind him and lives life according to the RTC ways.

Venis, like The Goodfather, was also a heathen. He actually had more repenting to do than his fellow RTC members, having supposedly been an actor in X-rated films. The former "porn star" would come to the ring dressed in only a bath towel and revealing shorts and eventually gyrated his way to two Intercontinental championships and one European title.

But Venis now leaves the towel and shorts behind, having found the "good life" in the ways of the RTC. He has realized that his ways of the past were immoral and that he needed to lead a healthier and more wholesome existence in order to set a better example for his fans and peers.

While Richards is the brains behind the morally correct operation, Bull Buchanan is the muscle. The former law officer will not let any one wrestler or faction "bully" the RTC around. He is ready, willing, and able to pound the RTC message into anyone who asks for it.

Even though Richards and his RTC members preach that they want to rid the WWF of all the bad influences, one has to wonder if this is really the truth of their ways. Are they really concerned with the minds, bodies, and souls of the wrestlers and fans or is there some other motive behind their censorship?

Is the RTC really using the product they're selling? Are they really as "moral" as advertised? Do they stand for the good of the federation or do they just want total control of the WWF? Think about it. This group is comprised of middle-card grapplers who were never really on top of the federation, and most of the wrestlers on their hit list are top contenders. If they rid the WWF of these so-called bad guys, who prospers in the end?

The fans definitely aren't buying what the RTC is selling. They boo the RTC whenever they enter the ring. But Richards and his army just ignore their greetings as they continue to fight the "good" fight because they know what is right and what is wrong.

Howard Kernats

Rikishi Phatu

Howard Kernats

You can bet your a$$ that this wrestler is not only going to be around for a long time, but(t) he's also going to do some damage to anyone who dares to step into the ring with him.

Born Solofa Fatu, this 6-foot-1, 421-pound grappler can wrestle with the best of 'em, coming as he does from a family with a rich wrestling background. He is the nephew of Afa the Wild Samoan, who was one half of the legendary and former WWF World tag champs from the eighties, the Wild Samoans. The Samoans also took time out of their busy schedule to train the young wanna-be wrestler.

Fatu would make his pro debut with another family member, his brother, known as the Tonga Kid in 1986, as The Islanders. He would then ply his trade overseas in Japan and then Montreal before making his way back to the States.

Now under the watchful eye of Buddy Roberts and paired with his cousin Samu as the Samoan Swat Team, Fatu won his first World Class tag team belt, beating Kerry and Kevin Von Erich on August 12, 1988. The fabulous duo would win another two straps before the year was out and would then be noticed and signed by the NWA.

While with the NWA, they feuded with several big-name tandems like The Midnight Express, The Road Warriors, and the Steiner brothers, Scott and Rick. They were also managed by none other than Paul E. Dangerously (Paul Heyman).

In 1992 the World Wrestling Federation came calling for the twosome. They would move on to the new organization with another family member onboard—Fatu's Uncle Afa was now their manager. One of the first things the duo did was change their name. They were now calling themselves The Headshrinkers.

The Headshrinkers would open some eyes and make a BIG impression on the federation at the 1992 Survivor Series, where they beat High Energy (Owen Hart and Koko B. Ware) on November 25. The tag team would get the victory when Fatu pinned Hart after a move off the top rope. As they were moving up in the rankings, they ran into one of their old rivals, the Steiners.

The Steiners would get the best of The Headshrinkers at WrestleMania IX on April 4, 1993, but that didn't stop them from making their way to the top. They would eventually meet and beat the Steiners again in their travels, and they would also take on and beat another awesome twosome, the Smokin' Gunns.

In 1994, with the help and guidance of their new manager, Capt. Lou Albano, The Headshrinkers would receive a much-deserved title shot. On April 26, 1994, the Shrinkers met The Quebecers and beat them for the right to be called World Tag Team champions. Again, Fatu scored the victory for his team with a move off the top rope when he nailed Jacques for the pin and win.

This would be one of the last highlights for the duo as they eventually broke up during the course of the next year. In 1995, Fatu decided to go out on his own and took on the ever-famous and tough King Kong Bundy. Impressively, the now-singles grappler beat his impressive foe on that night, August 12, 1995. Even though over the course of the year he beat good wrestlers like Rad Radford, Hakushi, and Hunter Hearst Helmsley, he couldn't move up in the rankings or billings.

In 1996 he became a fan favorite as an anti-drug crusader, who wanted "to make a difference" in the kids' lives. He would even meet and defeat the great Bob Backlund in the ring that year, but still couldn't get anywhere in the federation. He moved on and wrestled the rest of the year in smaller indy leagues.

In 1997 he returned to the WWF, under a mask and with a new manager, Backlund, grappling as The Sultan for a little while. He had a match at WrestleMania XII against Rocky Maivia (The Rock), in which he lost to the then Intercontinental champion. He wrestled on and off in the federation for the next two years, until 1999 when his ship to wrestling stardom finally came in.

He reappeared with a new look and costume—that's if you want to call a G-string that's two sizes too small for him a costume—along with blond locks and a new name. He called himself Rikishi Phatu and almost immediately he starting kicking a$$. He worked his way up the ranks and eventually the match that put him over was the one in which he scored a victory on a DQ on Smackdown! on January 4, 2000, against Triple H.

His dancing act with Scotty Too Hotty and Grand Master Sexay, otherwise known as Too Cool, was also going over BIG with the fans. Rikishi would face The Rock and, although he didn't win, he didn't lose either, since the match was declared a no contest in the end. He would meet and defeat the Big Boss Man several times when the big guy would make his first appearance at WrestleMania since 1997.

This was also a BIG night in Phatu's career, as he would be remembered not for what he did during his match, but what he did after his match. Rikishi gave baseball legend Pete Rose a Stink Face—his signature move where he sits atop the ropes in one of the corners and rubs his butt all over his unfortunate opponent's face. His sitdown piledriver has also become one of his most lethal weapons between the ropes, but it takes a backseat to the Stink Face.

His BIGGEST moment to date came at Fully Loaded, in a cage match against Val Venis when he dove off the top of the cage à la Jimmy "SuperFly" Snuka and came crashing down on his helpless opponent. This was a dangerous feat to perform for anyone, let alone someone who tipped the scales at over 450 pounds, but Rikishi didn't want to let his fans down.

"Yeah, I was trying to decide whether or not I was going to do it or not going to do it," he said in an interview with IGN Wrestling. "At the last moment, with 20,000 fans screaming their heads off, I had to do it or I'd let them down, and I damn sure wasn't going to do that."

Rikishi has mentioned time and time again how much he loves wrestling and how thankful he is to his fans. He realizes that without them, there would be no Rikishi Phatu to talk or write about.

"I love wrestling. It's not that I like it, I love it," he explained. "It's something that's in my blood. As long as I can walk to the ring, and I'm able to perform and make my fans happy, I'll do it. These people here make Rikishi. Rikishi doesn't make the fans. You know yourself, if the fans don't agree with you, you're going downhill. The fans call the shots."

BIG words from a BIG-time wrestling superstar.

Road Dogg

Howard Kernats

The Road Dogg is a wrestler who has bite *and* bark, and he has proven throughout his World Wrestling Federation career that he can throw down with the best of 'em. This 6-foot-2, 236-pound grappler has taken advantage of every opportunity thrown his way and has not only succeeded, but thrived. At one time in his career, his merchandise sales ranked third in the federation, trailing only The Rock and "Stone Cold" Steve Austin.

The Nashville native combined with Billy Gunn as The New Age Outlaws to win the WWF Tag Team titles on five different occasions. This duo was laughed at when they first entered the tag scene, but they would prove all the naysayers wrong by dominating the tag circuit and by copping so many championships. They became as feared on the circuit as they were successful simply by breaking the rules. The New Age Outlaws used this psychological advantage to their advantage, as their opponents were always anxious about antics when they met these two warriors.

The Dogg is a fan favorite who aims to please every time he steps into a ring. He works the crowd and mic about as good or better than anyone in the business today. And when he wasn't stirring up the crowd with his voice, he would stir the pot as part of the rebellious wrestling group DX.

This tough-as-nails wrestler has also proven himself capable on the singles circuit winning not only an Intercontinental belt in his career, but also being one of the pioneers of hard-core wrestling. He became the third wrestler ever to hold the Hardcore title as he won the belt in Spokane, Washington, on December 15, 1998.

Along with his toughness and skills, The Dogg's biting personality has kept him popular with the fans. But don't piss off this Dogg because he isn't your best friend. He's proven that many times over, most recently at SummerSlam in Raleigh, North Carolina, this past summer when he took on his good friend X-Pac in a match. Even though he lost the match to his DX friend courtesy of a low blow and an X-Factor, The Dogg proved that he could put the bite on anyone who got in his way, including his friends.

The Rock

Pics Pix

The Rock's path to wrestling stardom may be typical of today's grappling society, but it sure doesn't compare to times past when it would take years for a new wrestling character to catch on, let alone take over the industry!

The Rock, a.k.a. Dwayne Johnson, came onto the World Wrestling Federation mat scene in November of 1996. In four short years, Johnson has climbed and reached the top of the pro wrestling mountain, but all was not glorious during his trek to the top. The Rock wasn't always the good guy who could do no wrong in the WWF. As a matter of fact he wasn't even called The Rock.

But once Johnson got to the top, he knew how to stay there, as he "knew his role" in the industry.

"I think when you look at the character of The Rock, his first and foremost purpose is to entertain the fans like nobody else can," he said. But while he may know this today, he had to find out the hard way that the fans aren't always on your side.

Johnson was born into a wrestling family as the son of former NWA Florida and WWF Intercontinental Champion Rocky Johnson and the grandson of the legendary High Chief Peter Maivia. Even with wrestling in his blood, it was not Dwayne's first career choice.

The young Johnson grew up liking contact sports and excelled in one in particular: football. The gifted athlete was even voted a *USA Today* all-American football player during his high school years, which led him to a college scholarship to the University of Miami, where he played for four years. Although he had a solid college football career, even helping to win the National Championship in 1991 with the 'Canes, his campaign was marred with several injuries that held him back from playing up to his potential and being drafted by an NFL team.

When he went unselected in the 1995 NFL draft, he was still determined to make it to the pros so he decided to give the Canadian Football League a try, in hopes of one day being able to make his way to the NFL. He signed on with the Calgary Stampeders of the CFL, but again he would find the pro football door closed due to league rules restricting the number of non-Canadians who could appear on the active roster. Johnson was placed on the team's taxi squad—he was allowed to practice with the team but not play in games. As the season wore on, he began to feel that this sport wasn't for him and decided to give his dad a call. He now wanted to get into the family business—wrestling! Although his dad was unhappy at first about his son's decision to enter the lonely and brutal world of professional wrestling, he saw the fire and determination in Dwayne's eyes and decided that he himself would be the best person to get his son ready for ring action.

Eventually the younger Johnson received a tryout in front of World Wrestling Federation official Pat Patterson, and after a few tryout matches he was signed to a developmental contract with the WWF. He was sent down to Jerry Lawler's Memphis-based United States Wrestling Association and grappled under the name Flex Kavana. In no time, the future star was impressing the powers that be at the WWF so much that they recalled him and entered him in the Survivor Series in Madison Square Garden in New York City on November 16, 1996. Wrestling under the name "Rocky Maivia," a combination of his dad's and grandfather's names, the rookie won the prestigious tournament in his official debut.

This didn't go over well with either the veteran talent or the wrestling fans. They all wanted to know how this unknown could come along and steal the spotlight? What was irritating them even more was that he was a nice guy who smiled all the time, so how could they get mad at him?

Well, the fans showed in no time how easy it was for them! They grew sick and tired of Maivia's smiling, wholesome ways and began greeting him with "Rocky sucks!" cheers whenever he entered the arena. Some fans were even more harsh and chanted "Die, Rocky, Die!"

The fans were starting to resent Maivia. Here was a character who, yes, had family members who had once been in the business, but the fans didn't know this character from Adam and felt as though he was being shoved down their throats. They retaliated by shoving Maivia right back down the WWF officials' throats. They wanted to pick their so-called heroes. They didn't want to be told when to cheer and who to cheer for, especially for a character that was an undeserving, inexperienced pretty boy who had just came onto the scene.

At first, Maivia didn't know how to handle such crudeness, and when he went down with a knee injury he began to question his career change. He began to wonder if he had made the right choice. But he would find out soon enough that it wasn't the career choice that was wrong, it was his in-ring persona that so irritated the crowds and fans.

The WWF officials were also baffled by the fans' behavior; after all, Maivia was a good guy who was supposed to be on their side, so why weren't they on his? They would later learn that wrestling in this day and age is controlled by the fans, and the badder the battler, the better! And as soon as Rocky realized this, he took the ball and ran with it!

His first change came when he joined forces with the Nation of Domination, one of the WWF's biggest and baddest heel groups at that time. His next mission was to get back at the fans and scold them for not supporting him. Even though this was making the boos louder, it was making his reaction greater, which is what pro wrestling is really all about—stirring up heat with the crowd and other talent! The boos now felt great, as heels, unlike heroes, are supposed to be booed!

His efforts were so successful that he found himself right smack in the middle of a feud with the WWF's most popular babyface at the time, "Stone Cold" Steve Austin. He would challenge Austin to an Intercontinental title match, saying, "If you do accept my challenge, then your bottom line will say 'Stone Cold' has-been. Compliments of The Rock."

With that saying and that confrontation, Maivia emerged as The Rock, a self-confident, arrogant wrestler, who thought he was God's gift to wrestling and who was also constantly referring to himself in the third person.

His change to the badder was not only better, it also catapulted him into an area where he was quickly becoming one of wrestling's most recognizable personalities. But Maivia said his dad was not too happy with his son's choice of turning heel.

"All his life he's been a 'good guy' so he really wasn't too happy with that," The Rock said. "But then as the tides turned and I became more successful in the role as the man people love to hate, he applauded the decision."

At the time as the federation bad boy, The Rock so liked his role that he aspired to be the WWF's top heel. "I see myself being the top villain in the World Wrestling Federation," he said in an interview with Slam Wrestling.

His heel antics were not the only thing that was catching on with the fans. They also were now taking hold of his catchphrases and were echoing them when he entered the arena. The Rock had really gotten over in a big way in no time flat!

Claiming to be "The People's Champion" and "the most electrifying man in sports-entertainment," he would capture the WWF Heavyweight championship after winning the 1998 Survivor Series on November 15, 1998, against Mankind. This win would not only be the first of many world titles for The Rock, it would also start a feud between him and Mankind, since "The People's Champ" was being helped by the federation's boss, Vince McMahon, in his title win. The Rock had now turned corporate, and when the fans began to boo, he responded by telling them that they could "kiss his candy ass" for being against him in the past. He had now taught the fans a lesson and was well on his way to teaching the rest of the WWF a lesson in laying the smack down. No jabroni was safe or omitted.

In kicking jabroni ass, The Rock has not only risen to the top of the popularity list in wrestling, he has also found an audience outside the squared circle. He has made TV appearances on shows such as *Star Trek Voyager*, *The View*, *Martha Stewart Living*, and has also hosted *Saturday Night Live*, becoming only the second wrestler ever to be asked to do so. His image and eyebrow has also graced the covers of several mainstream magazines such as *TV Guide* and *Newsweek*.

"It does get overwhelming and I'm very humbled," The Rock said. "Who would have thought I'd be on the cover of *Newsweek* and *TV Guide*, hosting *Saturday Night Live*? It's harder to gain (mainstream success) because of the industry we're in. I think we've gotten over the stereotypical hump of 'is it real or is it not real?' It's sports-entertainment. It's physical theatricality at its best."

Speaking of the best, The Rock is currently the best face in the business. He gets the loudest pop and has the biggest following in the wrestling industry, and it's going to be interesting to see how it all pans out in the WWF now that "Stone Cold" Steve Austin is back in the ring. Could this mean another return to the dark side for "The People's Champ"? Only time will tell. The one definite is that the WWF surely smells what The Rock has cookin': the five-time world champ can lay the smack down with any candy ass in the business!

Saturn

Saturn is truly a wrestler from out of this world. Although he has yet to find his niche in the World Wrestling Federation as either a heel or hero, those are small obstacles for this ring warrior to overcome.

Outside the arena, Saturn has already endured the toughest battle of his existence—his childhood. According to an interview he did in the September 2000 issue of *Raw Magazine*, this Ohio native, experienced abuse as a child and endured days of hell so that what he does today for a living seems like child's play.

When he was five years old, he remembers seeing wrestling on TV and thought to himself that probably no one picks on those guys, and from that moment forward he wanted to be a pro wrestler. While the wrestling fans are the lucky ones, now having the bald warrior around to entertain them, Saturn was the true victim here.

While other children and wanna-be grapplers fall in love with wrestling for various different reasons like glory, fame, fortune, or the competitive nature of the business, Saturn was looking at the industry through different eyes—black-and-blue ones.

"I'm cross-eyed from the muscle damage done to my right eye," he said in *Raw Magazine*. "I've had two eye surgeries. They can't fix it. I'm tone deaf in my left ear from being hit on the head. That's why wrestling really appealed to me. I knew those guys were tough, and I decided it was what I wanted to do, too."

He grew up worshipping grapplers like Arn Anderson and Rick Rude, and it wouldn't be long before he was in the ring just like them, but he had a hard road to travel before he got to the squared circle. He would get into trouble early and often.

On one of these occasions, a local police officer, Ron Turner, lent the troubled kid a helping hand. He would teach Saturn martial arts after school to try and help the youngster not only learn how to protect himself, but also how to channel his aggression. Unfortunately it wasn't enough, as he got to hanging around with the wrong crowd and before you knew it, at the tender age of fourteen, as he told *Raw Magazine*, he was sentenced to four years in a detention home.

But at seventeen he was offered the opportunity to join the army and not only serve his country but he was also given a second chance to turn his life around. Although it was hard at first for Saturn to adjust to all of the army's rules and regulations, being a rule breaker not a rule follower, he more than made the adjustment. Of the one thousand recruits that signed up during his enlistment, only eighty-two made it to graduation day and, impressively, he was one of them.

But Saturn didn't just graduate, he excelled in his class during his time of service as an elite U.S. Army Ranger. He not only learned how to protect himself, but now he had learned how to function as part of a team. When it was time for him to return to life as a civilian, he was sky high, and for the first time in his life he felt like there wasn't anything he couldn't do.

"I loved the feeling of rising in the ranks," he explained, because as a child he was always told he was a loser. "As tough as the army tried to be, there was nothing they could do to me that hadn't been done already."

The first thing he did when he returned to everyday life in Cleveland was write a letter to the editor of a wrestling magazine to find out where he could learn how to become a pro wrestler. In reply he received the phone number to "Killer" Kowalski's wrestling school.

Saturn packed his bags and has never looked back. He is living proof that you can be anything you want to be in life as long as you want it bad enough, despite the trying circumstances.

In his case, it's not about winning belts or titles, it's about overcoming obstacles, and I don't mean the ones that stand 6 foot 6, 280 pounds. These obstacles are much bigger. As a matter of fact, they're immeasurable. When it comes to labeling this grappler as a heel or hero, there's no doubt in my mind that he's a capital H-E-R-O, hero. And even those letters don't come close to describing his achievements or being.

Scott Steiner

Howard Kernats

Better known around the wrestling circuits as Big Poppa Pump, Scott Steiner has really come into his own in the past year or so. In the ring, he not only looks good, he sounds good.

The former Michigan State Wolverine, who was a two-time all-American wrestler in college, has added an impressive mouthpiece of late to an already lethal wrestling arsenal. He currently is considered one of the meanest and most powerful grapplers in the WCW and both federation head honchos, Vince Russo and Eric Bischoff, have big plans for Poppa with him joining their New Blood regime in late 2000.

Steiner is not only an amazing wrestler, he also has a great story. Due to very serious back and shoulder injuries, he almost called it quits. In an interview with scoopswrestling.com in September 2000, Steiner explained that he'd almost hung up his trunks, when, after having surgery for the injuries, he couldn't even walk.

"It was real close," he said. "I was like that for six months. I had three ruptured discs, and I couldn't stand up straight. In fact, I came to New York because my buddy Jumbo Elliot, who plays for the Jets, he set me up with the guy who worked on Dennis Byrd (a football player who was injured and paralyzed with a spinal injury that occurred during a Jets game). He worked on me, took X rays. My spine looked like I had scoliosis. It's the way my body was trying to keep itself out of pain, you know? I went to him, but he couldn't do the surgery for two weeks, so I went to California to Dr. Watkins. They were good friends so I trusted him. Right after surgery I couldn't walk. Two or three feet and I felt like my knees were going to explode. It was a hard trip, man. Yeah, I really thought I was done. I was lucky I came back."

Correction, Poppa, the WCW and the fans are the ones who have been lucky.

Steiner has been known to take over whole shows lately with his mouth and his in- and out-of-ring antics. Last season, on a Nitro broadcast, he made six separate appearances, doing something different each time. One of the things he did on this night was challenge federation exec Vince Russo to a duel, another time he dared to take on Booker T while also having it out with his own flesh and blood, Rick Steiner. Speaking of blood, he would even duke it out with Tank Abbott on this night. When he wasn't picking a fight with someone on this broadcast, he worked the mic and crowd to perfection, boasting about his between-the-sheets action with Chiquira and Midajah.

This was all in one night's work for Pump. So much for his being done in the industry, Big Poppa Pump seems to have only just begun. Many in and around the WCW believe that Poppa is one of the ones that can bring the federation back to its glory days. They feel the 6-foot-2, 270-pound, chiseled grappler has his finger on the pulse of modern-day wrestling, and they wouldn't be opposed to having him carry them on his muscular back to the promised land.

Although his style is not what the WCW put up with in the past, as Big Poppa likes to curse and talk about his female fan club, the top officials seem to want to move in a new direction and follow in the ways of wrestlers just like Pump. Today, the wrestlers can't get by on just ring skills and moves anymore, they must also be blessed with the gift of gab. They have to know how to work a crowd as well as an opponent. They must be masters of disaster on the microphone. And Steiner brings all those qualities to the table.

All of these new qualities are what makes wrestling such a soap opera these days, but it also makes for great viewing and entertainment. Little did anyone know that this wrestler, who was known throughout the industry as a tag specialist along with his brother, Rick, would blossom into such a big singles star.

Steiner has not only won six WCW World Tag Team titles with his brother during his career, he also at one time used to work for Vince McMahon's WWF promotion, where he and his brother also found success by winning two tag championships. But even though he found success in the duo ranks, no one could have predicted the success that he has today. Yes, he was a good wrestler, there are no two ways about that, but he just didn't seem like the breakout type of wrestler who had not only the skills but also the savvy to go places,

Rick was the more charismatic wrestler. He seemed to have more of a ring personality than his brother. Scott just seemed like the guy who was all-business and no say. The grappler, who sometimes wore a U.S. flag type outfit kept to himself and did his talking in the ring.

But after proving everything that he had to on the tag circuit, he broke away from his brother and started hanging with the bad boys of the New World Order. He would also change his look at this time to the short, dyed-blond hair he still wears today, proving to everybody that blonds do have more fun and success.

Blessed with the biggest arms in the business, this blond-bomber has managed to capture three WCW U.S. title straps along with two World Television titles. He made an impressive showing on April 14, 2000, at Spring Stampede, winning the U.S. title tournament by defeating three rough-and-tough opponents in The Wall, Mike Awesome, and Sting.

This grappler, who is always escorted into the arena by a harem of gorgeous women, has the size, strength, and skills to be one of the game's greatest. Although he doesn't use it much anymore, he has one of the most lethal weapons in his back pocket in the Frankensteiner to go along with his signature Steiner Recliner.

No matter how you pump it, Big Poppa has the power to not only destroy anyone in the ring, he also has the ability to carry this federation into the future on his broad shoulders.

Al Snow

In Al Snow, the World Wrestling Federation literally created a "monster." What else can you call a wrestler who takes advice from a mannequin head and used to walk around with "help me" written backward in ink across his forehead?

When asked what brought this truly gifted athlete to this terrible mental state, Snow says that he became so distressed with the treatment he was receiving from the federation in regard to his in-ring persona and scheduled matches that he looked for someone who understood him.

Howard Kernats

The two would find each other (well, actually, Al found his better half one night amongst the trash in an undisclosed location while working for the ECW on loan from the WWF to the organization) and almost immediately other wrestling stars' heads began to roll.

Snow claimed that the head, which he simply called "Head," was the only one who appreciated his art, and that she was the inspiration for his success. And who was going to argue with a 6-foot, 234-pound professional wrestler who took instructions from a plastic head? Not Vince McMahon. Not any of the WWF superstars. Not the fans.

Snow has not only piled up victories in the ring, he has also won some gold along the way. He has three Hardcore belts to his name and one tag championship title with Mankind from November of 1999. The Hardcore straps kind of tell the story as to what type of wrestler this Lima, Ohio, native is. He is a ruthless and destructive force between the ropes, as Snow will do and use whatever it takes to get the win. He doesn't care if it's a chair, a trash can cover, the steel entrance ring steps—hell—he's even been known to give some good "Head" on occasion.

But no matter where the scouting tips are coming from, Snow has taken full advantage of his opportunities to become one of the most respected grapplers in the biz. Besides, just like the saying goes, "two heads are better than one," which is so very true in Al Snow's "mental" case.

Sting

Sting has been a WCW fan favorite and also an exception to the rule having remained with one federation his entire career. It is very rare in this day and age that a wrestler stays with just one of the big two what with the organizations having been in a ratings and talent war for the past ten years.

The face-painted grappler came onto the wrestling scene in 1987, and has remained loyal to World Championship Wrestling ever since. Another rarity is that he has also resisted the temptation to go over to the dark side of the business and grapple as a heel. He has given his heart and soul to the federation and has even lent a helping hand to up-and-coming wrestlers who needed some guidance.

One of the wrestlers Sting took under his wing for a bit was Vampiro. The longtime WCWer saw in Vampiro loads of potential and wanted to help the grappler reach his peak. Many were even calling Vampiro the next Sting. But this seemed to be a huge task, as Vamp was known to be a loner who didn't have many friends. The good thing about Vampiro was that he had proven himself capable in the ring against the bigger stars like Ric Flair and Lex Luger, but he just couldn't seem to come away with the victory that would put him over the top.

This is where Sting thought he could help out. He would show the kid the ropes and teach him the tricks of the trade that had helped him win so many prestigious titles in his career. He approached Vampiro, and the two hooked on as a tag team. Many saw only good things for this tandem as they had potential tag-team champs written all over them. This would also help Vampiro get over the hump and finally reach his stride.

Being the good guy that he was, Sting had nothing but good intentions in mind when he teamed up with Vampiro, but he would soon realize the hard way why this dark warrior had no friends. He would realize that the guy was meant to be alone and didn't deserve anyone's help.

On April 10, 2000, on a Monday Nitro telecast, Vampiro maliciously attacked Sting and broke up their partnership. He had just joined forces with the New Blood, a faction that was out to rid the WCW of all the so-called old blood. Although he was shocked by the incident, the 6-foot-2, 252-pound veteran didn't take the attack lying down. This would start a feud that brought out the best, or worst, in Sting. His actions began to resemble those from 1997, when he went off the deep end and mauled and brawled with everyone, from Hulk Hogan to the towel boy when Sting's own loyalty was questioned.

Although he has always been popular with the fans, Sting's recent association with Vampiro has taken him to new heights. He has taken his game to a new level, and his passion in the ring seems to have doubled ever since their paths crossed. While Vampiro and Sting may have made an awesome twosome and have many common traits, they also have many differences.

Howard Kernats

The scary-looking Vampiro comes to the ring in face paint like his former partner and makes mysterious appearances in the ring like Sting did in 1997, but unlike Sting, Vampiro couldn't give a darn about whether or not he gets cheered or booed in the ring. The eerie wrestler at one time even tried to sway Sting over to the dark side during their association. But Sting wanted no part of his Darth Vader–like world.

The two were now at war in classic Jedi knight and stormtrooper fashion.

The foundation for their bouts was not only revenge, but also good versus evil. But it wasn't your typical good guy–bad guy battle. There were some deep-seated issues here which bordered on the occult, but no matter, it still made for good wrestling.

While Vampiro acted like a heel was supposed to act, backstabbing Sting and torturing him whenever possible, Sting had given the face role a new look. Though he still got a tremendous pop from the fans, he had no problem with acting in heel-like fashion whenever he was in the ring with Vampiro. Sting may very well go down as the most sadistic hero professional wrestling has ever seen from this blood feud.

The six-time WCW World Heavyweight champion had taken it upon himself to club Vampiro with his trusty black baseball bat whenever he had the chance, and in turn Vampiro had done things like drag his foe through the ring floor and smashed a tombstone over Sting's head.

There were no limits to what these two would do to each other. It wasn't even about getting the win anymore. It became all about destroying the other guy's career.

Each time the two entered the ring to do battle, there was a certain feel in the air that the unexpected was about to happen. They gave the WCW an element it had lacked for a long time—must-see action—that it needed in ratings war with the WWF.

One of those must-see events came on June 11, 2000, at the Great American Bash in Baltimore, when Sting met his nemesis in a Human Torch match. Again, nothing was beyond the realm of possibility for these two gladiators, but this was way too dangerous. The flames brought new meaning to the phrase "helluva" match, with the emphasis on the hell! Like I said earlier, the matches between the two were no longer about wins and losses, and this one just happened to be about who put the other on fire first.

This was a match that Sting had no business being in as he was a proven champ who had already made a name for himself over the years; who didn't have to resort to partaking in gimmick matches to get over with the fans or management. But this was not about getting over. This was about not backing down. Sting was not about to lie down for anyone. He wanted good to conquer evil no matter the cost.

On this night Vampiro would get the best of him, getting the win by setting Sting ablaze. But history has proven that when Sting's buttons are pushed, he'll stop at nothing to get his revenge.

One other time in his career his loyalty and integrity were challenged, and he came out like a bat out of hell. At the time, Lex Luger had been attacked by someone who looked like Sting and rumors began to circulate that Sting himself had done the job, even though he'd had no time for such shenanigans as he was battling the evil wrestling faction, the nWo. This sent Sting over the edge and at War Games, the honest grappler turned his back on the WCW and seemed to be done with not only battling good vs. evil, but also wrestling.

But the following night on a Nitro telecast he made an unforgettable entrance, descending from the rafters into the ring. This would also be the first night the fans would see him in his new getup, being now costumed all in black with white facial paint, and wielding a black baseball bat. His new persona was an immediate hit with the fans!

His new philosophy was now to speak softly and carry a big stick! Only the new-faced grappler would do all of his talking with the bat, staying away from the mic and interviews for quite some time afterward; only appearing mysteriously and striking swiftly.

Where this battle leaves him, only the future will tell, but you can bet your last dollar that this "good guy" will not go away so quietly!

Lance Storm

Lance Storm is your typical badass foreigner who comes to an American-based federation to wreck havoc on as many Yanks as humanly possible. While this gimmick has been done many times before in years past, none seemed to have perfected the part quite as well as Storm has.

Howard Kernats

This 6-foot, 232-pound Canadian grappler learned the tricks of the trade, like his fellow countrymen Chris Jericho and Chris Benoit, from the legendary Stu Hart in his basement training ground, known as The Dungeon, back in Canada.

After finishing the grueling course at the Calgary-based school, Storm headed out into the wrestling world. His first opponent just also happened to be his first tag-team partner, Chris Jericho. The two teamed up to form a successful tag tandem known as The Thrillseekers. They would make a name for themselves on several independent circuits, especially the Smokey Mountain Wrestling organization, where the young duo competed against and beat several teams who had much more experience than they did.

Storm then took his act overseas, where he competed in Austria's CWA and Japan's WAR promotion, and managed to win three tag team titles along the way. When he came back to the States, he signed on with the Philadelphia-based Extreme Championship Wrestling, teaming with Justin Credible to form an awesome duo known as The Impact Players. The tag team would dominate their ranks for some time and would win championship gold in their together, but Storm knew he was wrestling on borrowed time at ECW.

He arrived on the World Championship Wrestling scene toward the end of 2000, and within weeks he was stirring the pot. This is quite an accomplishment for Storm, as he's not a very talkative wrestler, as he likes to have his in-ring action do his speaking. And believe me, his actions speak volumes.

While he has been known mainly as a successful tag wrestler throughout his career, Storm stormed onto the WCW singles scene and won the U.S. Title tournament on July 18, 2000, and immediately changed the title name to the Canadian Heavyweight Championship. A couple of weeks later on July 24, the grappler would face Big Vito in a Canadian title vs. Hardcore title match, in which Storm won and changed the title name to the Saskatchewan Hardcore International title. But he wasn't finished collecting titles or changing names there. Only days later, on July 31, the Canadian native won the Cruiserweight Championship from Lt. Loco and proceeded to change the name of that title to the 100 Kilos and Under Championship.

Even though his actions weren't popular with his colleagues or the fans, this chiseled grappler was surely putting his country's stamp on the WCW in the short time that he was a member of the federation. Modern-day wrestling is all about getting a reaction, positive or negative, and Storm was certainly getting reactions! Albeit not positive, they were causing a stir nonetheless and getting him noticed.

While he may not be able run his mouth the way several successful heels do, Storm truly lets his Japanese suplexes and aerial moves do the talking while he's between the ropes. Storm also may not have that many American friends here in the States, but who needs friends when you have titles?

Tazz

Tazz-mania came to the World Wrestling Federation during the 2000 Royal Rumble and has increased more and more with every match the former Extreme Championship wrestler takes part in.

Although he stands a mere 5 foot 9 and weighs 240 pounds, don't let his physical stature throw you off. Tazz is tough as nails and has an arsenal that can rival anyone's in the business. Brought up

Pics Pix

on the tough and mean streets of Brooklyn, New York, Tazz can come at his opponents with a German suplex, a side salto suplex, a vertical suplex, or one of his all-time favorites, the T-bone Tazz-plex. When all else fails, the stocky bone crusher resorts to his katahajimi Tazz-mission, which is usually a lock for him to get the win as his foes are usually gasping for air from the move, which is a cross between a choke and sleeper hold.

One of the WWF superstars who experienced the katahajimi firsthand was former Olympic gold medalist wrestler Kurt Angle. At Royal Rumble 2000 in front of a sold-out Madison Square Garden in New York, Tazz made his debut against Angle and would not only defeat his opponent in convincing fashion, he would also apply his "lethal" choke hold which seemed to knock the life out of Angle.

Many other wrestlers and WWF officials seemed concerned during and after this match as they had heard how dangerous Tazz could be in the ring, but now seeing it firsthand, they had no doubts in their minds that this guy came to play each night. The only problem is that his grounds for fun and games are a little more intense than some would like to see. As a matter of fact, it's borderline dangerous.

His intense competitive nature seems to have him in character twenty-four hours a day, seven days a week. Some wrestlers claim that when they're on the road, Tazz usually can be found alone, either working out in the gym or passing the time in his hotel room. The other grapplers try to find a way to relax and unwind, playing cards, going out to dinner, or just plain socializing with one another. Not the Brooklyn brawler. He seems to be on wrestling call every minute of every day.

Even on the day or night of his match in the arena, where many of the wrestlers get together backstage before their matches, Tazz can be found listening to his Walkman, stretching and warming up in some isolated area of the venue until he has to enter the ring.

Then, when it's his time to go on, he plows into the arena and takes on his opponent with every ounce of energy in his body. He truly wrestles like the Looney Tunes character, The Tazmanian Devil, as he usually takes down his foes in a lightning-quick, swirl-like fashion. But even though he makes quick work of his opponents, each and every move has a purpose. His game plan is one that is well thought out. Tazz wants nothing more than to be the best, and he knows that in order to do that, he has to be ready to beat the best.

Many wrestlers develop their game around only a few moves, and when they're in the ring they usually dance and prance around until it's time to apply them. Not Tazz. He's already played the match over and over in his head a hundred times before it actually takes place. Usually nothing takes this wrestler by surprise.

No one doubts that he can compete with the big guns of the game like The Rock, Triple H, and Steve Austin, but what they do fear is that this guy could seriously hurt one of the federation's top talents with ease. He has been said to have the vicious streak of Jake "The Snake"

Roberts, the shoot-fighting skills of Ken Shamrock, and the technical know-how of Bret Hart.

Put that all together and you have one of the meanest wrecking crews of a wrestler around in Tazz.

Too Cool

Too Cool is a World Wrestling Federation tag team that is—as advertised—too cool. Scotty Too Hotty (Scott Taylor) and Grand Master Sexay (Brian Christopher) not only combine to be one of wrestling's most dominant duos on the scene today, they also have danced their way into the hearts of the WWF fans.

Taylor has been with the WWF since the early nineties, but was never a major role player until he met his tag partner in 1997. Taylor would job in lesser matches in the federation, never really entering the spotlight. But in 1997 the organization decided to hold a tournament to crown its first ever light-heavyweight champion, and Taylor threw his hat in the mix.

In the second round of the tourney, he met up with Brian Christopher. Even though Christopher came away with the victory on this night, the two would meet over the next few months in what became a heated rivalry.

Before Christopher met up with Taylor in the light-heavy event, he had been a star in the United States Wrestling Association in Memphis for years. In 1997, the WWF officials took notice of his talents when he participated in several inter-promotional matches.

But the tag magic didn't surface until 1998, at WrestleMania XIV. The two grapplers were paired together in a tag-team battle royal and the chemistry was instant. The only thing that has changed over the years is their team name. After their WrestleMania performance, they dubbed themselves Too Much. They would wrestle occasionally over the next eighteen months, leaving an impressive trail of victories along the way.

Pics Pix

Russell Turiak

The Rock is a wrestling hero who lays the smack
down on any candy ass in the business!

Lita, Trish Stratus, and The Kat have proven that women are no longer just arm candy in the world of pro wrestling!

Howard Kernats

Howard Kernats

Howard Kernats

When you hear the sound of glass breaking in the arena, you're sure to hear the masses go wild as the meanest S.O.B. in wrestling, "Stone Cold" Steve Austin, garners more cheers than jeers from the crowds.

Russell Turiak

One of the most stylin' dudes outside the ring, Booker T also never disappoints with his snazzy maneuvers between the ropes.

Russell Turiak

Howard Kernats

"Big Poppa Pump" Scott Steiner and Buff Bagwell once paired up in the WCW and broke every rule imaginable—along with some necks, legs, and backs!

Howard Kernats

Kurt Angle would love to place some gold around his waist to match the medals around his neck.

The Walls of Jericho come tumbling down when Chris Jericho enters the arena.

Adam Copeland has a certain "edge" in the ring.

Who knows what goes on in the head(s) of Al Snow?

Howard Kernats

The Big Show shows that it's okay for a grown man to cry.

Howard Kernats

Russell Turiak

David Flair has the unfortunate privilege of trying to follow in his dad Ric's footsteps—as a top-notch wrestler, as well as a ladies' man.

Russell Turiak

Kane and The Undertaker give a new meaning
to the term "Blood Brothers"!

But with so much up-and-coming talent in the tag ranks, the tandem decided to tweak their image. Scott "Too Hot" Taylor became Scotty Too Hotty and Brian "Too Sexy" Christopher became Grand Master Sexay, and if you thought that was too much, Too Much became Too Cool.

Their image change would pay off as they not only became fan favorites, they also would win their first tag-team title on May 29, 2000, in Vancouver, against Edge & Christian.

Along with their rotund friend Rikishi, Too Cool has moved and grooved their way to superstardom. When the lights go down, the fans know that the tandem is about to bust some heads or bust some moves. But win, lose, or draw, Too Cool will definitely hear the cheers from the crowd. They are, plain and simple just Too Cool for words.

Triple H

Howard Kernats

On April 2, 2000, Hunter Hearst Helmsley, better known as Triple H, achieved what no other heel in the history of WrestleMania had ever done before—he walked away with the belt as the WWF World Heavyweight Champion. He had showed millions of people that good guys do finish last!

Throughout his tenure as a World Wrestling Federation badass, Triple H has leaped over all the hurdles and opponents thrown his way, proving once and for all that he is wrestling's all-time greatest heel.

Ever since its inception in the eighties, WrestleMania has not only been the Super Bowl of professional wrestling, it has also been the gauge to judge whether or not a particular wrestler had what it takes to be over with the audience, especially the World Heavyweight title holder. Vince McMahon will not hand over that belt if he's unsure of the talent winning it. After all, the WWF champ is the main personality by which his federation is judged, so he's not going to let just anybody win it!

But this time the decision wasn't going to be that easy. Yes, he was still the owner of the federation, but now every member of his family had a say in the outcome of the matches, especially this one. This was going to be a WrestleMania where the family was divided. Vince would have the WWF's meal ticket, The Rock, in his corner. His wife, Linda, had the WWF crowd pleaser, Mick Foley, in hers. Shane sported the federation's giant, The Big Show, on his side, and Stephanie was 100 percent behind her husband, Triple H.

But was the family really that divided on this night? For the millions who tuned in, it made for good TV, or Pay-Per-View in this case!

Helmsley's talents and mettle were really going to be tested on this night as he was pitted not only against three of the toughest grapplers in the history of the federation (The Rock, Mick Foley, and The Big Show) at WrestleMania 2000 in a Fatal Four Way Elimination match, but more important, his in-laws.

In the week leading up to the event, no one was giving Triple H a chance of keeping his title. The Rock was the fan favorite and most logical choice as Hunter and the "People's Champion" had been battling throughout the year with one another, and it would have been only fitting for the good guy to unseat the bad guy for the heavyweight strap. Also, with The Rock being the WWF's most popular wrestler and a babyface, it just seemed too perfect a situation to ignore. Oh yeah, and as I mentioned above, he also had the WWF owner on his side.

The next logical choice was Mick Foley. Foley and Helmsley have badass history behind them, as each of their matches was one slugfest after another, with Hunter usually coming away with the victory. This would have been sweet revenge for Foley to beat his nemesis in front of millions of his loyal fans. He was also on the verge of retirement and what better way for the WWF to pay homage to a grappler who put his life on the line each night for the federation. Foley was the underdog everybody was rooting for and had a chance of going out on top.

No one was really giving The Big Show any chance either, but he had an ace in the hole in having Shane in his corner. With Shane 'O Mac by his side nothing was beyond the realm of possibility. Shane was the type of guy The Big Show needed watching his back, as the boss's son had the reputation of doing whatever he had to do in order to get the victory—even if it meant going against his family.

So the deck seemed stacked against Helmsley that April night in Anaheim, but Hunter proved to everyone that he was up for the task. The knock-down-drag-out, no-holds-barred war saw The Big Show get knocked out of action first, followed by Foley, leaving good versus evil, The Rock against Triple H, to duke it out for the right to be called champion.

In a shocking turn of events, when it looked as though Hunter was going to fall to The Rock, Vince turned heel on the popular wrestler and assisted Helmsley in getting the pin and win. McMahon cited that he did it for his daughter and family's sake that night, but the guess here is that Mr. Mac thought that Triple H was deserving of the honor.

But Hunter didn't become the greatest heel by being good in the ring. He got his name because he has proven throughout his career that he will stop at nothing to achieve his goals. He likes to kick ass, not kiss it. He has also has the uncanny ability to hook up with the right people at the right time.

This is especially true when it comes to his female partners in crime. His first piece of arm candy was the ninth wonder of the world, Chyna. The fearless lady had backed Helmsley in all his shenanigans, and if anyone tried to get in his way, she would be there in a moment's notice.

Together they helped form one of the most lethal posses in the history of wrestling in D-Generation X. This would prove to be a very important association for Helmsley in his career, as DX, known for their rude and crude behavior, was over big with the fans and this put Triple H constantly in the limelight. So having Chyna by his side helped get him over with the fans and also helped him get by certain opponents on certain nights.

The other arm candy in his life that helped Triple H get to where he is today is none other than Stephanie McMahon. Although the legitimacy of their "marriage" is still a topic of discussion, what with the video clip of him and a passed-out Stephanie riding through a drive-through wedding chapel in Vegas is still fresh on everyone's mind, there's no doubt that Stephanie will stand by her man through thick and thin.

A perfect example of that fact came right after the showing of that clip when Hunter introduced the wrestling world to his new wife, and Vince vowed to get revenge on the sneaky villain. Hunter agreed to square off with Vince in a match that, if he lost, he would have to divorce Stephanie, and the match would speak volumes about Hunter's influence on his now-wife. During the December 1999 Pay-Per-View show, when Vince was about to strike his son-in-law with a sledgehammer, Stephanie ran into the ring and stopped her dad from slugging Hunter, claiming that she wanted the pleasure of doing it herself.

But the daughter of the boss dropped the hammer and Triple H picked it up and nailed her father for the win. Just when it looked like Helmsley was going to strike his wife also, he stopped and smiled and the two lovebirds gave each other a beautiful hug, right after they had double-crossed the elder McMahon.

With his five championship belts, and surely more to come, Triple H has reinvented the role of the heel in wrestling and has gone on to become the best bad guy to ever grace the mat. He is the villain the fans love to hate, and just remember, without heels like Triple H, there are no heroes.

The Undertaker

Howard Kernats

The Undertaker has been making his presence known ever since he came onto the World Wrestling Federation scene at the 1990 Survivor Series. But the 6-foot-10 grappler has done more than survive in his ten years between the federation ropes. As a matter of fact, this "Bad Ass" wrestler has been involved in some of wrestling's most memorable matches in his illustrious career.

The dark warrior engaged in a fight for the ages on October 5, 1997, in a Hell in the Cell square-off against "The Heartbreak Kid" Shawn Michaels. The Pay-Per-View was dubbed Badd Blood, and the title seemed to fit the match the two grapplers were going to take part in that infamous night.

Months earlier, "The Heartbreak Kid" had served as a guest referee for The Undertaker and Bret Hart in a match for the WWF championship belt. All throughout the contest, Hart provoked Michaels, causing him to swing a chair at "The Hitman." This action would hurt The Undertaker in more ways than one. Hart would duck under the swinging chair, causing the 'Taker to get nailed and pinned almost at the same time. Michaels had cost him the belt and win, and The Undertaker wanted revenge. He couldn't ask for a better setting to take out his frustrations on his foe, as the cell match consisted of the two men fighting in a ring enclosed by a sixteen-foot steel cage.

Neither wrestler would have any place to run and that's just how The Undertaker wanted it. He was used to matches that involved hellish surroundings and circumstances, so this was just what the voodoo doctor ordered for him. He would go to work on HBK as soon as the bell sounded. Michaels tried to mount an attack against his enormous opponent but nothing seemed to be working. It looked as though it was going to be a night of sweet revenge for The Undertaker, but it wasn't to be.

When a cameraman was injured inside the ring, the locked entrance to the cell had to be opened to let the injured man out. Michaels tried to take advantage of this opportunity and darted for the opened gate, only to be thwarted in his efforts by The Undertaker. In the process The Kid's face was plastered into the side of the cell.

With his face busted open and the cage now relocked, Michaels tried to escape his dark foe by scaling the cage, but The Undertaker was right behind him and the two then began to battle on top of the cell. As HBK tried to retreat back down the side of the cage, he was knocked off onto an announcer's table, and it seemed only a matter of time before The Undertaker took the victory. When he was about to pin Michaels after leveling him with a vicious chair shot, the unexpected happened; The Undertaker's brother, Kane, showed up and ripped open the cage. He then tombstoned the dark warrior, causing him to lose the match. Although he did not win, The Undertaker did get his revenge on Michaels by rendering him a bloody mess on that night. And his two friends Hunter Hearst Helmsley and Chyna had to carry him back to the locker room.

Another Hell in the Cell match that will go down as one of wrestling's bests occurred on June 28, 1998, in Pittsburgh, when The Undertaker duked it out with the masked grappler, Mankind.

While this match didn't contain the action of the Michaels-'Taker cell fight, it did have its key moments that have people to this day scratching their heads, not believing what they witnessed. The fans who were in attendance and even those watching at home knew they were about to see an historic event even before the match had started. Man-kind, a.k.a. Mick Foley, was making his way with chair in hand right to the top of the cage.

When The Undertaker was introduced and saw his opponent sixteen feet above the arena, he didn't hesitate to scale the cage and meet Foley on top. Upon arriving there, The Undertaker was greeted with two monstrous chair blows from Mankind. He would return the favor in a crazy way, launching Foley sixteen feet below onto an announcer's table. The crowd was silent and Mankind lay almost motionless for about three minutes until the paramedics and doctors rushed onto the scene. The Undertaker took all this in from his perch above the arena, still on top of the cell.

Just when it seemed the match was over, with Mankind being wheeled off on a stretcher, Foley jumped up and made his way not only back into the arena but back on top of the cage! Not knowing when to quit, Mankind was then thrown right through the top of the cage, down onto the mat sixteen feet below, by The Undertaker, and this time there was nothing to break his fall. Again he would lay motionless, but again Foley would get up and go at the dark angel, even managing to sprinkle the ring floor with thumb tacks. But The Undertaker would have the last laugh, nailing Mankind into the tacks twice before finishing him off with a tombstone piledriver.

But that was the old Undertaker. Today, there's a newer, badder, and bolder version of his character in the WWF—a modern-day 'Taker if you will.

This modern-day "Bad Ass" appeared on the scene at Judgment Day 2000, in stunning fashion during a Triple H vs. The Rock Ironman match for the World Wrestling Heavyweight title. In a crazy all-out sixty-minute match that had Shawn Michaels as the guest referee, Shane, Stephanie, and Vince McMahon at ringside, and DX involved in the ring action, The Undertaker would steal the show on this night as he came riding down the aisle on his motorcycle to Kid Rock blasted music and a thunderous crowd ovation.

Although the crowd roared in appreciation for their longtime su-perstar, they all stared at the grappler, not because he had been missing in action for almost a year, but because he now had a new look. No longer was he dressed in an eerie all-black outfit, he was now sporting a biker's getup, wearing dark sunglasses and a bandanna around his head. A look that plainly stated—BACK OFF!

That's what everyone should have done that night at Judgment Day as The Undertaker, now known as "The American Bad Ass," kicked some pretty good butt in the ring. He showed everyone in attendance that night that he was ready to be a prime-time player once again. He was now back to claim what he felt was rightfully his before he'd left, the top-dog spot in the federation. Also equipped with a new finishing maneuver, "The Last Ride," he was ready to take on anyone who wanted to give the "Bad Ass" a try.

And if he feels like it, the three-time WWF Heavyweight Champion might go after another title belt; after all, when you're an "American Bad Ass" you pretty much get to do what you want.

As the 'Taker said in an interview in *WWF Magazine*'s October issue, "I've always stood on my own and done what I wanted to do and have either reaped my rewards or taken the consequences."

Mostly the take-no-prisoners wrestler has reaped the rewards as he's battled and beaten some of the game's greats. Over the course of his career, he's gone toe-to-toe with the likes of "Stone Cold" Steve Austin, The Rock, Hunter Hearst Helmsley, Big Boss Man, Shawn Michaels, Bret Hart—hell—he's even fought his own flesh and blood, his brother, Kane, in the ring. There are no limits and no one that can stop him when he's determined.

"I don't care if it's Vince McMahon, I don't take orders from anybody," he said.

Spoken like the true Bad Ass that he is!

Vampiro

Howard Kernats

Vampiro is one man who takes his job so seriously that he takes it home with him. For some people this may sound crazy, but you have to understand that Vamp, a.k.a. Ian Hodgkinson, is no ordinary guy or wrestler.

This grappler's look is one-part Marilyn Manson and one part Dracula. Some have accused him of stealing his gimmick from The Undertaker or Gangrel of the WWF, and when he was asked about these statements in the December 2000 issue of *Wrestling World* magazine, he had this to say: "I don't have to 'out vampire' anybody. There's no parallels between Undertaker and I. I am a punk rocker into zombies, aliens, and vampires. I don't think you live until you're dead. I know Gangrel very well. We went to Japan together (to wrestle). All these little whining kids who complain I'm a rip-off of Gangrel should know he's a friend of mine.

"I think what I do is 100 percent different from what anyone else does because I don't act. . . . I've always been a vampire. Anyone who's a fan of horror and wants to be a vampire, great, but you can definitely tell who's acting. Just because you give somebody some fangs and a ruffly shirt, and they roll their eyes back in their head, that doesn't mean shit! The way you see me now is the way you would see me at 10 o'clock at night at McDonalds . . . I would never want to be Undertaker or Gangrel. I'm Vampiro. Those guys copied me!"

Hodgkinson was born in Ontario, Canada, where he quickly picked up on the country's national past time, hockey, and excelled at the sport. The young hockey star would eventually be drafted by the Montreal Canadiens and play half of a season in the Kingston Ontario League, but left to pursue his childhood dream of becoming a pro wrestler.

In 1984, the punk rock–loving dreamer hung up his skates for a pair of wrestling boots. With forty bucks in his pocket, he left home, took a bus to a wrestling show in the Montreal area, and approached Abdullah The Butcher about getting started in the business. At first the wrestling icon couldn't be bothered, but then gave in when he saw how determined Hodgkinson was. The Butcher made the kid an offer he couldn't refuse: in return for helping the crew set up the ring and selling programs, he would let Hodgkinson sleep in his truck and would teach him how to wrestle. The legend then took a liking to the gracious student and taught him some ring psychology and how to take bumps between the ropes.

Just when it looked like the kid from Canada would make his debut, the organization folded. Before parting ways, the Butcher gave Hodgkinson the address of a wrestling company in Mexico, but it did him no good at the time because he had no money to get there.

A struggling-actor friend from Montreal would come to his rescue. The friend, who was now living in Hollywood, bought him a one-way ticket to L.A. This would not only help him get closer to Mexico, but Hodgkinson would also get his first taste of gothic blood. Despite having a decent job as a doorman at a club called Rubber, which was owned by actor Mickey Rourke and singer Billy Idol, he was known as a "Hollywood vampire" due to his lifestyle of living on the streets and roaming the city after dark.

Hodgkinson would eventually scrape up the money to get to Mexico, where he looked up the wrestling federation Abdullah had told him about. He arrived in Mexico City on New Year's Eve, 1989, with a hundred dollars to his name. He hooked on with the EMLL and CMLL wrestling federations and before you knew it he was a star. Because of his look and fondness for vampires, he was given the ring name of El Vampiro Canadiense.

While wrestling in Mexico, he locked horns with Konnan and the two became bitter enemies. But this feud didn't stop him from becoming an overnight celebrity in Mexico. He not only starred in the ring, but also on TV. While down there, El Vampiro even got to pursue his love of music and was also a hit on the rock 'n' roll stage.

In 1998, he gave up his Mexico celebrity status for the rings of the WCW. Even though he toiled around jobbing in lesser matches, he didn't complain. He sat back and waited for his turn in the limelight, which was kind of unusual for a vampire, but hey, we're not talking about an ordinary wrestler here. He would make his debut in the federation on March 18, 1999.

He started out as a heel, but instantly caught on with the fans, which oddly turned the dark character into a face. But the fans' love for him wasn't only because this guy was good or bad in the ring, it was because he took the time out to show he cared outside the ring. He showed that he was gracious of their support and that he didn't mind giving back.

"I am not into the limo scene," he explained. "I still ride the subway. I got my bicycle. I still skateboard, and I take the extra hour to hang out after the shows to sign everything the fans ask me to whether it's raining, freezing, whatever. I hang out. I've always been me, I've always been cool. I never thought of Vampiro as a big star. I come from a very humble family, a very poor background, and I am very grateful for what I have. I bleed wrestling."

Recently, the WCW had the grappler paired with Sting and it looked like they were going to be together for a long time—until Vampiro turned on his partner, again playing the big-time heel role. On playing the role of heel he had this to say: "I have always been a babyface. People in Mexico used to say I had an angel on my shoulder because the fans liked me, and I am very uncomfortable being a heel because I really love entertaining people, I really love being the underdog."

Vampiro, who has more than sixty tattoos on his body, plays the underdog role so well because he's been one all his life. While some may think that he's hiding his identity behind all his face paint, it's the true Vampiro fan that knows he'll never deny or forget where he came from.

"When I'm painting my face and I'm listening to really hard-core music and looking at my tattoos," he said, "I'm thinking about those days on the streets. I'm in pain before I even get down the aisle. Then I see the fans approving of me. It's almost like I'm always saying I'm sorry. I feel so guilty that I've done bad things in my life. So when the fans cheer me, I'm humbled. I still walk the same as I did back then. My feet are still on the ground. I'm still walking on Sunset Boulevard."

The Dark Angel got the attention of wrestling fans all over when, at the Great American Bash, he took down Sting in a blaze of glory in a Human Torch match on June 11, 2000. While this may have been extreme, it didn't matter to him as long as he was entertaining the fans and working his way up the ladder.

Vampiro is definitely one of the most talented wrestlers in the industry today. He not only can handle himself between the ropes, he also knows how to get over with the fans. He started out positioned as a bad guy, but the fans turned him good by their reaction. You can't get much more popular than that.

X-Pac

Howard Kernats

X-Pac is living proof of two things in wrestling. Number one, you don't have to be a 6-foot-6, 280-pound, chiseled-out athlete in order to succeed in pro wrestling, nor do you have to remain the same character throughout your career to be able to get over with the crowd.

Obviously X-Pac is not close to being 6 foot 6 or 280, but he still is one hell of a wrestler. He first appeared on the World Wrestling Federation scene in 1993 on a Monday Night Raw telecast as the clean-cut grappler the 1-2-3 Kid. When the fans and the other wrestlers got a look at this scrawny "kid," they immediately passed judgment. In their eyes, this guy didn't belong in the WWF. Hell, he didn't even belong in the business.

But the Kid would prove them all wrong. Armed with an aerial assortment of maneuvers, he would gain the wrestlers' respect and the fans' support by taking on and beating grapplers who were much bigger than him. The young gun would also find success as a part of a Kliq that included Shawn Michaels, Triple H, Diesel (Kevin Nash), and Razor Ramon (Scott Hall). And when Hall and Nash jumped shipped to wrestle with World Championship Wrestling, the Kid wasn't far behind his warrior friends.

He would wrestle in the WCW as Syxx, the sixth member of the newly formed federation wrecking crew, the New World Order. After causing all kinds of havoc in the ring, he would return to the WWF with this newly found attitude as X-Pac, a loud obnoxious wrestler who sported a scraggly beard, a raggedy bandanna, and dark glasses.

X-Pac would latch on with some other federation rebels, Michaels, Triple H, and Chyna, and form a hell-raising group known as D-Generation X. The Minneapolis native would crotch-chop his way to two European titles and four tag-team titles, taking on any and all in his way. The rebellious grappler was known around the circuit for not only challenging wrestlers two times his size, but also for his low-blowing, cheating, and interfering ways.

At one time or another he has crossed paths with Triple H, The Undertaker, Gangrel, and most recently Chris Jericho, who he viciously attacked with nunchaku on several occasions.

More victories and titles are surely in the cards for this talented grappler, and if you don't believe that, well, in X-Pac's words, you can just "suck it!"

Beauties
Amongst Beasts

Who's got bigger "Gunns" than Big Poppa Pump? Who's more Hollywood than Hogan? Who can melt the ice from "Stone Cold"'s veins in a stunning minute? Who can play more mind games than The Game himself, Triple H? Who's sexier than The Big Sexy? And who cooks up more heat in the wrestling kitchen than The Rock? The gorgeous women of wrestling—that's who!

These sultry vixens of the ring have risen to the top of the wrestling world over the past couple of years faster than Goldberg has disposed of his opponents. They are no longer there for *just* their looks, as these lovely ladies have shown that they are not only often the brains behind the brawn, but that they can also handle themselves in the ring.

They have recently broken down some barriers in sports-entertainment and are now a voice that can be heard. The women are popping up and out all over the wrestling circuit and are holding titles and positions that many thought would never be possible in this male-dominated industry.

In 1999, Chyna became the first woman wrestler to compete in both the King of the Ring tournament and the Royal Rumble. Although she didn't win either event, she let the men know that she was ready, willing, and able to compete on their level. The chiseled warrior queen would turn some heads when she won the Intercontinental title from Jeff Jarrett in October 1999 at a No Mercy event.

Not long ago, a wrestler would walk into the arena accompanied by a man who was referred to as his manager. In a like manner, a woman would perform the same task and be labeled a valet. Not anymore! Times sure have changed on the mat scene. While some chauvinists still have a problem letting a female manager run their career, most grapplers welcome the possibility. Last year in the WWF, Edge & Christian battled The Hardy Boyz in a match for the right to call Terri Runnels their manager.

The female personalities come in many shapes and sizes in all the major promotions. The WWF sports babes such as Terri, Chyna, Ivory, Jacqueline, The Kat, Debra, Lita, Stephanie McMahon, Tori, and Trish Stratus, while the WCW has its share of leading ladies in Miss Hancock, Major Gunns, and Torrie Wilson.

Each lady brings something different to the ring every night for her federation, but you can be sure that they will play an even bigger role in the entire sports-entertainment field in the years to come. The beauties amongst the beasts have given an entirely new meaning to the term "knockout" on the squared circle circuit.

Chyna

Chyna, the Ninth Wonder of the World, made her WWF debut in 1997 as the bodyguard of Hunter Hearst Helmsley. No one anticipated that she would ever evolve into anything more than the back-watching role she was working at the time, but over the years, Chyna has proven all her skeptics wrong. Way wrong.

She has paved the way for other women looking to make it big in the wrestling business, and she has also shown that she's capable of tangling not only with other women in the ring, but more impressively, that she can battle and beat the best males in the federation.

Pics Pix

When Chyna a.k.a. Joanie Lauer, first accepted the job as bodyguard for Helmsley, she guarded her man (who, by the way, is her real-life boyfriend) with her life. When Helmsley was feuding with Goldust, who was managed by his then real-life wife, Marlena, Chyna and the golden one's spouse went at it just about as much as Helmsley and his rival. Many thought that that's where Chyna's role would lie, feuding with the valets/managers of Triple H's opponents. But boy did they underestimate this gifted goddess!

Before long, Chyna would be mixing it up with top wrestlers such as The Undertaker, "Stone Cold" Steve Austin, and Goldust. She would also become one of the founding members of the WWF Gang, D-Generation X. This opportunity helped her career greatly as not only was the 5-foot-9, 185-pound beauty the posse's only women representative, she also got more exposure with DX being in the limelight on a weekly basis.

Chyna was now not only knocking on doors, she was breaking them down. In 1999, she became the first woman wrestler to compete in both the King of the Ring tournament and the Royal Rumble. Although she didn't win either of the prestigious events, she sent a message to her male coworkers: she was seriously capable of playing with the big boys!

In October 1999, Chyna put her money where her mouth was and not only beat one of her male counterparts, she also garnered her first championship title. At a No Mercy event in Cleveland, Ohio, the Ninth Wonder of the World left Jeff Jarrett wondering how the hell she beat him for the Intercontinental belt. Since that first strap victory, Chyna has gone on to win the IC belt two more times.

Chyna has paved the way for women to not only be able to work in the wrestling world, but more important, to be looked upon as equals. Amazingly the chiseled grappler has never held the women's title in her career. She has been on a mission from day one to prove that she could do battle on the same platform as the men, and so far, she has made them sit up and take notice.

Aside from her in-ring successes, Chyna has also become a household name outside of the WWF. The Killer Kowalski–trained wrestler has been a presenter on the MTV Music Video Awards; she has her very own comic book, where she plays a super hero–like character; and she has been a guest star on TV shows such as *Pacific Blue*, *Third Rock from the Sun*, and *The Tonight Show with Jay Leno*. She also attended the Democratic National Convention to help promote the WWF's SmackDown Your Vote voter-registration campaign.

The end of 2000 has seen Chyna introduce to the world her exercise video entitled *Chyna Fitness*, and she has revealed herself completely to her fans in both the November 2000 issue of *Playboy* and her autobiography, *If They Only Knew*.

As an on-line guest for Playboy's Web site one evening, Chyna spoke about her breakthrough appearances in the mainstream and her posing for the premier men's magazine.

"I think by doing the things that I have done on television and by posing for *Playboy* magazine, I've really broken the ice for a lot of other women to look how they want to look."

But one of the accolades she would like to one day have in her possession is the WWF's World Heavyweight title, though she doesn't know if she or the public is ready for it just yet.

"I would love to be world champion," she said. "I don't know if the world is ready for a female champion, but if there was one, I would like it to be me. It wouldn't matter who I fought. It would be more the principle of holding the title."

And if ever there was a woman capable or worthy of holding pro wrestling's most prestigious belt, it's certainly Chyna.

Debra

Howard Kernats

Although she was away from the mat scene for quite some time nursing her real-life boyfriend (who is now her husband) "Stone Cold" Steve Austin back to health from major surgery, Debra is back and, before you know it, will reestablish herself as one of wrestling's premier women of the mat.

Before she left the wrestling scene, Debra was clearly the top dog (or puppy in her case) on the women's circuit. She not only knew how to get it done in the ring, as she won the women's title on May 10, 1999, in Orlando, Florida, but she was also the best manager hands down (or shirts off) doing whatever it took to get her man the win—even if it meant showing off her curvaceous body.

What makes Debra so valuable as a manager is that she has the confidence in her ability to know everything there is to know about every wrestler in the WWF, and her beliefs become embedded in her wrestlers' brains and carry over into the ring. She has the ability to mold champions and distract the opposition at the same time.

Debra made a brief appearance on Monday Night Raw on October 9, 2000, when she ran into Chyna backstage and asked the Ninth Wonder of the World to point her in the direction of Commissioner Mick Foley's office. Chyna obliged and welcomed her former coworker back. The blond bombshell then made her way to Foley's office to clear up the rumor that had been circulating around the wrestling world that she had "run down" her hubby, Austin, with a car several months back.

Once inside, Foley asked her if she had run Austin down because she was sick and tired of the WWF superstar being away on the road. Debra explained to Foley that there was no way she had run "Stone Cold" down, as she loved her man too much to hurt him.

How she is eased back into the WWF picture is up to the powers-that-be, but once this shrewd businesswoman is either back full-time in the ring or managing from outside the ropes, you can bet your bottom dollar that she'll become a major presence again in no time. And that's the bottom line because Mrs. "Stone Cold" says so!

Major Gunns

After starting out as one of the nWo girls who would parade around the ring with Jeff Jarrett, Tylene Buck has now found herself with a "major" role in the World Championship Wrestling federation.

The California native, a professional model by day and wrestler by night, made her ring debut on May 15, 2000, when she appeared at ringside with the Misfits in Action group led by the scandalous Captain Rection. The Misfit leader introduced his newest recruit to the wrestling world as Major Gunns.

In only her second week on the circuit, Gunns used her "ammo" to help out her teammates, distracting Ralphus on a May 22 Monday Nitro long enough for Sgt. Stash to perform a dirty deed. This was also the first night that the Misfits asked the Major to perform mouth-to-mouth on one of the WCWers. From here on in she would have the responsibility to administer the emergency procedure on any injured (and willing) grappler.

But Buck has proven that she can administer more than just mouth-to-mouth. She can also more than handle herself in the ring thanks to training sessions with Madusa at the WCW Power Plant training facility in Atlanta. Madusa took her and several other grappling gals under her wing and taught them not only how to take bumps in the ring, but also how to execute several wrestling maneuvers to perfection.

These instructions would pay off for Gunns as she quickly became one of the WCW's "major assets." Over the course of her ring career, Gunns has attacked and feuded with some of the biggest women on the wrestling circuit. Her infamous battle with Miss Hancock even had the WCW thinking about bringing back the women's division, as the two sexy wrestlers were receiving as big a pop from the crowd as some of the popular male wrestlers.

When this beautiful blond is not throwing down in the ring, she can either be found gracing the covers of several magazines such as *Ironman, Pump, Truckin',* and *Muscle Sport,* or she can be found on the pages of various calendars and catalogs such as *V. W. Bikini Team, Soda Sweethearts, Sport Truck Magazine, Max Muscle, LoveLace of Hollywood, Wicked Temptations, Psychotic Wear, Legendary Rock,* and *Sex Wear.* Buck has also appeared in her share of videos such as *Ironman Magazine Swimsuit Spectacular* numbers 3, 4 and 5, *Hot Rods & Hot Bods,* and the Maxerciser Infomercial.

Howard Kernats

Miss Hancock

Howard Kernats

Miss Hancock, a.k.a. Stacy Kiebler, is a very deceiving young lady. Ever since she burst on the WCW scene when she won a Nitro Girl Talent Search Contest in November of 1999, she has made a habit of misleading the audience.

Kiebler would win the dancing girl contest and come onto the circuit as a new Nitro member who went by the name of Skye. Winning this contest was no big stretch for Kiebler, being a former professional cheerleader who had once displayed her pom-poms on the sidelines during Baltimore Ravens games. But the wrestling world would soon find out that this sexy blond was not in it just for the exposure and dancing, but more for the ring competition.

Kiebler took it upon herself to start showing up ringside at the matches of Leni & Lodi, two wrestlers who were under the watchful eye of a pro-censor group. With a clipboard in hand and a sexy librarian outfit and nerdy glasses, she called herself Miss Hancock and pretended to be a moral crusader on behalf of Standards & Practices. But in reality, the 5-foot-11, curvaceous sexpot was really present just to stir the pot and get some quality airtime.

The audience soon realized that Miss Hancock was no quiet, shy librarian. In fact, Hancock loved to strut her stuff on top of announcer tables, bumping and grinding her way into millions of homes and hearts each week on Nitro.

The not so prim and proper bombshell took her act into the ring where her she would do a different kind of bumping and grinding with her fellow women personalities. Hancock seems to love the action between the ropes and has proven to be quite a competitor. She even took part in training lessons from another WCW female grappler, Madusa, at the federation's training facility, in Atlanta.

The sessions, which were twice a week for eight hours, have turned Hancock from pretty to pretty lethal. Although she expected the consultations to be physical, Hancock said in an article in *WCW Magazine* that she hadn't expected to be hurting once they were over.

"I came home the first day with bruises all over me," she said. "I watched wrestling and thought the mat was bouncy and padded, but it's not that way at all. It does hurt."

The leggy blonde has put all that behind her and instead of her feeling pain, she now concentrates on hurting her opponents. In her short time on the mat, Hancock has battled with some of WCW's top gals: Daffney, Major Gunns, and longtime federation favorite, Kimberly.

But the eyebrow-raising siren doesn't seem to care who she faces in the ring because she's ready, willing, and able to mix it up with whoever wants a piece of her. Hancock has proven that she's not the reserved lady that some believe her to be. From match number one in her wrestling career, she has shown that she is more about kicking butt than revealing it.

"It was against Kimberly, and I think I surprised a lot of people who thought I was prissy because of my character," she said. "But I came out there in my high heels and kicked her ass."

And from the way it looks, she will be doing plenty more ass kicking in the future.

Ivory

Ivory is a woman on the World Wrestling Federation circuit who is a competitor first, eye candy second. She was responsible for revitalizing the women's division and, in the process of her bringing back interest to the group, she has captured two WWF women's championship titles.

Before coming to the WWF, Ivory got some experience and exposure with another wrestling organization, which is now defunct. She wrestled for GLOW (Gorgeous Ladies of Wrestling) as Tina Ferrari

Howard Kernats

and found some success on the circuit. While there, she captured the top prize of federation champion, and when the organization closed up shop, she took a hiatus from wrestling to pursue a career as a makeup artist for Revlon.

But she would soon miss her time on the mat and the rush that came with in-ring competition, so she decided to not only come knocking on the WWF's door, she more impressively knocked it over, not caring who was behind it. The powerful, sexy warrioress has the skills and experience to take the division to heights it has never seen before. And if all goes according to her plan, Ivory will do it sooner rather than later.

Jacqueline

Jacqueline not only has killer looks, but also killer moves on the mat. The sexy grappler has proven time and time again to her fellow female wrestlers not to mess with her between the ropes.

The former Miss Texas isn't afraid of anyone on the circuit and has the reputation as the strongest and most athletic female on the World Wrestling Federation roster. She has won two women's championships so far in her career, and there's certainly more gold in the future for the bronze bomber.

She has ignited quite a few sparks on the WWF scene. Jacqueline was once linked with the female grappler Sable's husband, Marc Mero, in a storyline that snowballed into a battle of the ages. The women would tangle not only for the women's belt, but also for the affections of Mero. It made for great action and TV.

Jacqueline, who is also known to throw down with the men on the circuit, was once aligned with Terri Runnels, and they pranced around the ranks as PMS (Pretty Mean Sisters) alongside Mark Henry and D'Lo Brown stirring up things in the federation.

But make no mistake about this rough and tough female, when it comes to action, she's right in the middle of it. Jacqueline has the strength and athleticism to not only dominate the women's ranks, but to also mix it up on the men's circuit. There is no man or woman who could hold her back from succeeding in the pro wrestling ranks.

The Kat

The Kat came into the federation as a lost kitten who would follow all of Chyna's ways, from her jet-black hair to her jet-black leather ring attire. But those days are long gone as The Kat has proven herself to be a kitten no more. As a matter of fact, she's more often associated with "puppies" these days than felines.

Originally, she had started in the wrestling business courtesy of her real-life sidekick, Jerry "The King" Lawler, who had introduced her to the physical confrontations of the ring. The Kat, a.k.a. Stacy Carter, got her start with stints in

Howard Kernats

Power Pro Wrestling, Music City Wrestling, and also the National Wrestling Alliance, as Lawler pulled some strings to get her in.

But by 1999, after taking her lumps and bumps in the smaller federations, Carter made her way to the World Wrestling Federation as a manager. She was associated with Debra McMichael and Jeff Jarrett for some time before the crowd really took a liking to her as the miniversion of Chyna, known as Miss Kitty.

But the wrestling tigress has abandoned that persona and taken on a role where she not only gets over with the crowd, but also on her competitors in the ring. The Kat can claw with the best of them, and she already has two women's championship straps to her credit.

In August 2000, The Kat proved to the wrestling world that she was ready to take on any and all who wanted a piece of her. At SummerSlam in Raleigh, North Carolina, she squared off against Terri in a Stink Face Match. Not only would The Kat "face" her opponent on this night, she would also nail her with some other pretty impressive moves in the ring. On one occasion, she gave Terri "head" when Al Snow threw his mannequin head to her in the ring and she smashed Terri in the face with it. In other instances, The Kat pulled off a body slam and a bronco buster on her curvaceous foe.

The Kat has the purr-fect makeup for success on the women's circuit. She has the looks, the moves, and the know-how to get what she wants. And all indications point to her wanting to hold on to the women's belt for a long time to come.

Lita

The WWF has one of the hottest women in all of pro wrestling in Amy Dumas, a.k.a. Lita. The fiery redhead has taken the wrestling world by storm as she is not only about sexy looks, she also has smashing moves.

Lita can not only wrestle with the "big girls" on the pro grappling scene, she can also throw down with the "big boys" of the mat. She has a wrestling arsenal that's the top of the heap on the women's circuit, combining high-

Pics Pix

flying aerial maneuvers such as moonsaults and hurracanranas with a judo background. Her repertoire is even the envy of some of the men in the federation.

Dumas admits to not being a wrestling fan growing up, but when she caught a glimpse of the Mexican grapplers working their magic one night on the tube, she became hooked on their lucha libre style. The impressed young woman was so hooked that right from that very moment she wanted to fly as high as those guys were. Dumas knew she wanted to be a pro wrestler, and she didn't fool around when it came to learning the high-flying style either. She went right to the source: she packed up and moved to Mexico.

Her first attempt in 1996 saw Dumas making some progress as she got to know some people on the Mexican circuit and even got to do a few little vignettes and a spot as a manager, but when her money ran out she returned to the States. However, her new contacts in Mexico promised to train the up-and-coming grappler if she ever returned to their country.

With that in mind, Dumas saved and saved until she had enough cash to return and eventually made her way back to Mexico for a three-week crash course in the lucha libre style of wrestling. After Mexico, she moved on to Chicago where she had some wrestling contacts who were also willing to train her.

When these two-a-day sessions were over, Dumas decided it was time to put her training into action, and she went looking for work on the indy circuits. While wrestling in the indy ranks, she ran into a duo who would impact her career then and who would also play a major role in her success today, The Hardy Boyz.

"They were on an indy show that I did very early on—my third show with Mid-Atlantic NWA [National Wrestling Alliance]," she explained in an interview in the September 2000 issue of *Raw Magazine*. "I got to talking with them and they invited me to come down and train. I worked a lot of indies in North Carolina, so I would work down there and then go over to their ring on Sunday to train."

She claims to have learned a lot from Matt and Jeff Hardy and also credits Shawn Michaels and Triple H for having a great impact on her style and career. It didn't take very long for her to start a buzz on the independent circuit and by the spring of 1999, Dumas was working for the ECW, where she plied her trade both as Angelica and Miss Congeniality.

She would also enroll in Dory Funk's wrestling dojo for a week, where she honed her skills some more. Funk had been responsible for helping wrestlers such as Test, Edge & Christian, Val Venis, and Kurt Angle, and the young grappler was hoping he could also teach her some tricks of the trade.

Funk did become a major player in helping get the talented wrestler noticed. The teacher showed a tape of his new student to Bruce Prichard, who happened to be the VP of Talent Relations for the WWF, and by October 1999, Dumas was working for the federation. Although she would wrestle in only dark matches with Essa Rios for some time, it didn't take too long for the fans and other wrestlers to notice what she could do in and above the ring.

She burst onto the main scene in February 2000 as Rios's valet, Lita, and made headway and heads turn from there on out. Lita eventually broke free from Rios and went her separate way. And since their separation, her popularity has risen to unimaginable proportions. When Lita enters the ring, the crowds go wild.

She has taken bumps with not only the baddest women on the circuit, but also some of the meanest men. Paired with The Hardy Boyz, this trio puts on a better aerial show than the United States Air Force.

But in the short while she has been in the WWF, Lita has proven that she doesn't need to ride the coattails of any grappler, especially a man, in order to be successful. On August 21, 2000, Lita proved just how successful she's capable of becoming when she won her first women's championship title in style over the owner's daughter, Stephanie McMahon, with The Rock being a special guest referee.

This women's title was only the beginning for this bona fide super starlet. It won't be long before this sexy siren is the "Lita" of the pack for women wrestlers all over the world.

Stephanie McMahon

It comes as no surprise that wrestling's biggest heel on the men's circuit, Triple H, is "married" to wrestling's biggest heel on the women's circuit, Stephanie McMahon.

The daughter of the federation boss is not only beautiful and intelligent, she is also one of the biggest rebels in the federation today. She has proven time and time again that she knows what and who she wants and will stop at nothing to get either.

Since she first came on the scene in 1999 (as part of a kidnapping plotline), she has not only played with the careers of many of the federation's stars, she has also clashed with each member of her family at one time or another. She once stood by and watched Triple H nail her dad with a sledgehammer and walked away from a stricken Vince arm-in-arm with her hubby.

Her brother, Shane, was next on the hit list as his little sister once slapped him on a Monday Night Raw. At the time, Shane was concerned with how the federation was being run under the guidance of Stephanie and Triple H. It was also no secret that Shane didn't like his brother-in-law who, a week earlier, had nailed the heir apparent to the WWF throne with a metal chair.

On March 6, 2000, in Springfield, Massachusetts, Shane was in the center of the ring with The Big Show and was ranting that he didn't like Triple H, and he accused "The Game" of brainwashing his sister into wearing slutty attire. All of a sudden, Stephanie appeared on the scene and slapped her brother in the face.

But the unbelievable happened on a March 23, 2000, SmackDown! when Stephanie said that there would be an announcement that night that "would knock the WWF off its foundation." Vince's young daughter then proceeded to invite her mom into the ring and would go on and on about how she had been "mistreated" as a child. How she only got the regular edition of a sports car when she was sixteen instead of the turbo model. Or how she "only" got one hundred dollars a week while she was in junior high school. She then went on to say that she agreed with her husband that her mom was a conniving bitch. After that disparaging remark, the unappreciative daughter then proceeded to slap her mom in the face, adding injury to insult.

She has most recently turned her marriage upside down by becoming involved in a love triangle with Triple H and Kurt Angle, causing both warriors to battle each other for her affection. Although she has defended her "relationship" with Angle, claiming it's platonic, one has to wonder if her affections for the Olympic hero lie somewhat deeper. After all, Stephanie did turn on her own family for her "husband," so who's to say that she would not do the same to him for Angle?

Stephanie has proven that she can do whatever she wants, whenever she wants, in the federation. True, she has held the WWF Women's

Howard Kernats

Terri Runnels

Although Terri Runnels is not as active on the mat as some other women in the WWF this by no means takes away from her power and influence in the federation. Runnels is one of the most sought-after managers on the circuit. She has been known to take up-and-comers and mold them into champions almost overnight. As a matter of fact, two young, talented tag teams Edge & Christian and The Hardy Boyz battled it out at one time in a "Terri Invitational Tournament" to see which duo would have the privilege of having Terri as their manager.

The Hardy Boyz wound up winning her services, but they soon found out the hard way that if you don't stand up for and respect the beautiful manager, you're going to lose her. The Boyz lost her services due to their failure to protect her from another set of boyz, The Dudley Boyz, who plowed Terri through a table one night. An emotional Runnels left the side of The Hardyz after they let Buh Buh Ray powerbomb her, and she can now be seen working the sidelines for another up-and-comer in the federation, Saturn.

Known as Marlena when she first came onto the WWF scene, the woman directed the career of Goldust (Dustin Runnels), her real-life husband at the time. She has since ended not only her ties with the gold grappler in the ring, but outside as well. The two have separated and have gone their disparate ways both professionally and personally.

But in regard to her professional tactics, she is second to none. She usually doesn't have a literal hands-on approach to overseeing her partner's career, as her specialty is psychological warfare, but don't bet against her in the ring either.

Terri was battling it out with The Kat last year. The two vixens went at each other on several nights in all sorts of matches to try and iron out their differences. Whether she is distracting her opponents with her God-given gifts or throwing down in the ring, Terri has proven to be one of the most powerful females on the wrestling circuit.

Trish Stratus

Trish Stratus brings new meaning to the term T&A as she has aligned herself with the wrestlers Test and Albert. Not only has she given the monstrous duo the sexual innuendo as their moniker, she has also shown them, and others, a thing or "two" about the grappling business. Stratus took the tandem to new heights when she led them to WrestleMania to take on Al Snow and Steve Blackman, but more impressively, she guided them to a victory over the hard-core, lethal pair.

Speaking of grappling, the 5-foot-4, 118-pound bombshell isn't afraid to get tangled up in the ring either. She will do whatever is nec-

Howard Kernats

essary for her or her wrestlers to get the win. At anytime this fitness model will reach into her arsenal bag and pull out a trick or two. Don't let her size fool you: she isn't afraid to take on anyone. Trish won't think twice about getting in the line of fire and clotheslining a 6-foot muscle-bound opponent if it means getting the victory.

She has clashed with some of the top women in the biz, including Chyna, and although they may tower over her, this Toronto native can more than hold her own. She's tougher than she appears. She certainly proved her toughness on the night she was given wood by The Dudley Boyz as they plowed the helpless Stratus through a table during a match. She may not have walked away that night from the painful incident, but she came back better and more determined than ever to succeed in the rough and tumble world of sports entertainment.

Trish Stratus has all the tools to not only be a head turner, but also a headliner in the wrestling business. And she'll gladly take every opportunity to show what she's got.

Tori

You want athletic? Tori's athletic. You want tough? She can be that, too. You want beautiful? How about drop-dead gorgeous? But if you're looking for someone that's just around to be some guy's arm candy, you're barking up the wrong wrestling tree when it comes to this grappler.

The talented diva first came onto the WWF scene as an obsessed fan who would show up at arena after arena around the country to take in her favorite superstars, especially Sable. But not long after that she would show her

Howard Kernats

wares in the ring and take on any and all in her way. Whether male or female, this tough cookie didn't care, she just wanted a fair chance to make a name for herself.

And that she has. Tori has proven over time that she'll stand toe-to-toe with anyone in the federation. She was once aligned with Kane and had the guts to leave his side and shack up with his once best friend, X-Pac. But her most impressive feat to this day is when she turned the tables on Buh Buh Ray Dudley and plowed him through a table.

The vicious vixen got revenge on the deranged Dudley for once depositing her through the wooden piece of furniture and said in an interview in the October 2000 issue of *Inside Wrestling* that she enjoyed every minute of it.

"I didn't act like some helpless woman and go crying to the officials," she said. "I took matters into my own hands. I climbed that turnbuckle and put that fat blob Buh Buh Ray Dudley through a table myself."

Tori is a former bodybuilder who met "Rowdy" Roddy Piper in her hometown of Portland, Oregon. He took her under his wing and trained her for the mat wars when he found out she was interested in breaking into the biz. Before coming to the WWF, Tori graced the mats of the LPWA (Ladies Professional Wrestling Association) as Terri Power and proved in no time that she was the roughest, toughest competitor on the circuit.

The tough-as-nails beauty claims to have gotten into the business not for the fame and fortune, but more so for the competition. "I got into wrestling because I wanted to perform in the ring, Other people get into wrestling and jump at every (other) opportunity," she said.

Tori's aggressive style has put her in a position to challenge any female, or male, who wants a piece of her, but they should learn from the Dudley experience that "thou shall not mess with Tori!"

"I'm always aggressive," she said. "I don't let any man or woman shove me around, treat me like a second-class citizen or rough me up. Anyone who messes with me had better be prepared for the consequences."

Torrie Wilson

Torrie Wilson may have the body to become wrestling's next irresistible goddess, but in the ring the Boise, Idaho, native has the personality of a snake. Having been raised on a farm it's no wonder she gets along with animals—The Filthy Animals that is!

The sexy blonde was initially brought into the WCW by Kevin Nash and Hulk Hogan to charm David Flair into joining the nWo. She succeeded in her mission and lured him into the organization, but then "fell" head-over-heels for the young wrestler.

Wilson then would accompany her man, who was U.S. champ at the time, into the arena, proudly cheering him on from ringside. But

Howard Kernats

189

when Flair lost the belt, Torrie lost interest and in typical snakelike fashion, she slithered over to another young grappler, Billy Kidman.

She aligned herself with Kidman and his pack of partying rebels, The Filthy Animals, but soon enough she lost interest and reemerged on another young gun's arm at a Bash at the Beach event. This time it was "The Franchise" Shane Douglas.

With her looks and charm, she should set the wrestling world on fire in the near future, but she should also be very careful with her constant changing of loyalties because when you play with fire, you're bound to get burned!

Legendary Heels
and Heroes

Believe it or not, the heels and heroes of today obtained most of their personalities and gimmicks from the greats of the past. If you ask Hulk Hogan, he'll tell you that his wrestling persona is based on the traits of the legendary "Superstar" Billy Graham. Mick Foley, a.k.a. Mankind and Cactus Jack, patterned his style after one of his wrestling idols, Terry Funk.

These men understood the grappling philosophy that in order to have a successful hero, you also need a superstar heel. One cannot make it without the other. The players of the past also understood that they couldn't keep the same personality their entire career, so it wasn't beyond any of them to either turn heel or hero when their persona was no longer getting over with the crowd.

Heels and Heroes takes a look at six of wrestling's biggest legends from the past and takes you back over their careers when they either played the heel or hero role to perfection. Read on to find out more about Andre the Giant, Terry Funk, Bruno Sammartino, "Rowdy" Roddy Piper, "Superstar" Billy Graham, and George "The Animal" Steele.

Check out what these memorable matsmen brought to the ring each night and how they entertained their fans during their glory days. Also, take notice how they impacted the current grapplers on the modern-day circuit to become the superstar wrestlers that are entertaining you today.

Andre the Giant

A ndre the Giant was not only a giant in his time, his legacy still lives today.

The towering titan came onto the wrestling scene in 1971, appearing on the Canadian circuit under the Jean Ferre moniker. By the time The Giant was in his early twenties, he had wrestled all over the world, grappling in matches in South Africa, Morocco, England, Tunisia, Algeria, Scotland, and many more locales. But the 7-foot, 500-pound warrior didn't really become a household name until Vince McMahon, Sr., took control of his appearance schedule later in his career. McMahon took one look at Andre and knew that he had a winner on his hands.

"My initial reaction was 'My god, I never saw such a man,'" the late great wrestling promoter said in an interview with *Sports Illustrated* magazine in 1981. "I'd seen photographs and videotapes, of course, and I knew Andre was 7 foot 4 and over 400 pounds, but I simply wasn't prepared for how he looked up close. He was unlike anything I'd ever seen before, and I knew he could become the number one draw in wrestling."

McMahon wasn't fooling around when he said he could make Andre number one. As a matter of fact, during his time, The Giant became not only a household name when it came to wrestling, but also in the entire sports world. At the time, Andre the Giant was as popular in the sports world as Muhammad Ali.

Speaking of Ali, Andre took part in a boxers vs. wrestlers event in 1976, which was held in Shea Stadium in New York. The two legends didn't face each other that night in the ring. Ali went up against Japanese legend Antonio Inoki and The Giant faced boxer Chuck Wepner. The

Ali/Inoki bout wasn't too memorable, but the Andre/Wepner match lived up to its billing, as The Giant took hold of his opponent in the third round after Wepner had just landed his best punch of the contest (which would also be his last) and hurled him over the top rope, quickly ending the bout and any question as to who was the better man that night.

Andre didn't think the boxer stood a chance against him. "After all, a man may hit me a couple of times, but if I cut the ring off and close in, what can he do after I put my hands on him? The boxer has no chance since he can't even wrestle in a clinch because of his gloves."

But gloves or no gloves, no one ever really stood a chance against the enormous grappler. The man was unbeatable throughout his career. It wasn't until wrestling's next big star, Hulk Hogan, came along that The Giant actually lost a match.

As was always the case with Hogan, the Hulkster beat the giant grappler in stunning fashion, not only pinning Andre in front of 92,000 people at WrestleMania III in the Silverdome, but he also picked up his 500-pound foe and slammed him to the canvas.

But Andre would get his revenge on Hogan. The Giant would not only make a heel turn at this stage of his career, he would also beat the Hulk on February 5, 1988, on prime-time television on NBC live from Indianapolis, for the World Championship title.

Over his career, Andre proved that he wasn't a sideshow freak. His skills in the ring were as good as, if not better than, most of his opponents'. Yes, obviously he towered over his foes, but he was also a student of the game who was willing to learn new moves to add to his repertoire. His first promoter, Frank Valois, recalled in the *SI* article how Andre worked hard at his craft.

"He was trying so hard always," Valois said, "and anything the other guys could do Andre thought he should do also. In that first year or so he was around seven feet tall, and he weighed 325 to 350 pounds, but he looked skinny because of his frame. I'm telling you, he broke up some rings and ring ropes learning to do dropkicks and use the ropes right."

Andre the Giant would not only perfect his moves, he would also instill fear in the hearts of wrestlers all over the world who dreaded the thought of being in the same ring with the gigantic wrestler. But these grapplers didn't fear Andre for his size, rather they feared being out-maneuvered or, even more embarrassing, outwrestled by the Hall-of-Famer. He brought an excitement to a match that was second to none. He was truly in love with what he did for a living, and it showed in his work on the mat.

"Many men were afraid to go in the ring with him, especially after he reached his twenties, because he was so large and strong," Valois said. "For all his height and weight, he could run and jump and do moves that made seasoned wrestlers fearful. Not so much fearful that he would hurt them with malice, but that he might hurt them with exuberance."

For all the hurt he laid on his opponents, the number can be mul-tiplied one hundred times over to compare to the amount of smiles this mountain of a man put on people's faces. WCW tried to bring back a bit of his legacy when they billed a modern-day grappler Paul Wight (currently known as The Big Show with the WWF) as Andre's long-lost son and appropriately called him The Giant. But the gimmick never went over with the fans. Andre the Giant was not only one of a kind, but also a true hero.

Terry Funk

Terry Funk is really a modern-day warrior. It's tough to decide where his career capsule should go—with the modern-day wrestlers or with the legends of the game—ultimately the living legend belongs with the greats not only because of his skills and toughness, but also because of his uniqueness and longevity.

The 6-foot-1, 247-pound Amarillo, Texas, native made his pro debut on December 9, 1965, against Sputnik Monroe and is still going strong to this day. At fifty-seven, he is the oldest active competitor in WCW history, and there seems to be no slowing him down.

Funk is a second-generation grappler who, along with his brother, Dory, Jr., was trained by his dad, Dory, a legend in his own time on the Texas circuit. The Funks followed in their dad's winning ways and became the only brothers in NWA history to have ever held on to the World Heavyweight crown.

Terry won his first NWA World title from Jack Brisco in a best of three falls match on December 10, 1975, and he would successfully defend his title for two years before dropping the strap in February 1977. Over the course of his reign, he would not only meet and defeat other grappling greats such as Harley Race and Brisco, but he would also square off against his own flesh and blood, his brother Dory.

In the eighties, the Funkster also met up with the flamboyant Ric Flair, and their matches were also something to be remembered. The two would go toe-to-toe for the NWA title several times, and it was reported that Funk would even break his foe's neck on one occasion.

Funk gained a following and legendary status with his hard-core style between the ropes. He was introduced to barbed wire matches while he plied his trade overseas in Japan with the FMW, IWA, and Big Japan promotions. You name the organization, the WWF, the WCW, the ECW, Funk has not only wrestled there, he has prospered. He was hard-core before there was a hard-core division. As a matter of fact, he won the Hardcore title at Spring Stampede on April 16, 2000, in Chicago, against "Screamin' Norman Smiley", thirty-five years after his professional debut.

Over his illustrious career, Terry Funk has proven that he is not only a survivor, but more importantly a winner. He has accomplished more in wrestling in his fifties than most grapplers do in their entire careers. Throughout his professional life, the mat maniac has been an inspiration to hard-core wrestlers such as Mick Foley, and like fine wine, Funk just seems to get better with age.

Howard Kernats

"Superstar" Billy Graham

"**S**uperstar" Billy Graham lived up to his billing his entire career. And he surely was a true superstar on the mat. The 6-foot-3, 265-pound grappler was a noted rule breaker who took on anyone who wanted a shot at him.

Before becoming successful in the wrestling ranks, he'd made a name for himself in the weight room and on the bodybuilding circuit. The young, chiseled athlete got started pumping iron at an early age, which would lead him to win the first of his many titles, Mr. Teenage America.

His devotion in the gym not only led him to develop twenty-three-inch arms and a fifty-six-inch chest, it also led him to enter the world of professional wrestling. A graduate of Stu Hart's Dungeon in Calgary, "Superstar" would make his mentor proud, going on to become a World Heavyweight championship title holder.

Graham would win the title in stunning fashion as he squared off against the legendary Bruno Sammartino in the spring of 1977, in Baltimore, and beat the fan favorite in a highly controversial bout. The noted rule breaker would hold on to the belt for almost a year, sometimes defending the strap six times a week during his reign. He would eventually drop the belt to another up-and-coming star, Bob Backlund.

Over the course of his career, "Superstar" Billy Graham not only became one of the most feared and famous heels in the biz, he also became one of the most recognizable wrestlers of our time due to his strut and arrogance. Graham claims to have taken some of his shtick from Muhammad Ali, while Hulk Hogan credits most of his character's makeup to the antics of Graham.

"Rowdy" Roddy Piper

Pics Pix

In order for there to be heroes, there have to be heels and "Rowdy" Roddy Piper will go down in history as one of the all-time great bad boys. He could stir the wrestling pot as good as, if not better than, anybody in the history of wrestling.

Hot Rod made his debut in 1972 at the tender age of fifteen in Manitoba, Canada, and just four years later he would capture the first title of his career in a match held in Olympic Stadium in Los Angeles, California. Before coming to the NWA, he made stopovers in the Pacific Northwest promotions, honing his ring and mic skills along the way.

While in the NWA, Piper would square off against some tough competition, going nose-to-nose with Ric Flair, Ricky Steamboat, and Greg Valentine. Then in 1984, he landed in the WWF, where he would become a household name almost overnight as Hulk Hogan's chief rival. As the host for the popular grappling forum "Piper's Pit," Roddy proved himself not only to be rowdy, but also a good interview on the mic. Piper became the man the fans loved to hate back in the days of "Hulkamania."

He was a huge part of the contingent that brought the Rock and Wrestling connection to its high point in the eighties. His heel character was just as important to the rise and popularity of the industry as Hogan's hero character.

Piper has retired and come back to the sports-entertainment scene many times over, but the fans never seem to tire of his winning ways. Whether he's in the ring throwing down with the other grapplers, behind the mic, or behind the scenes, "Rowdy" Roddy will always be a voice that's heard and listened to, as the fans love to hate this ever-popular wrestler.

Bruno Sammartino

When you talk about the true good guys of the mat sport, Bruno Sammartino's name is always one of the first that comes to mind. In a like manner, when you speak of the greats of the game, his name also surfaces. He is truly one of the greatest good guys to ever set foot on a pro wrestling mat.

Sammartino not only was an international legend, as he grappled his way all throughout Europe and Japan, he also made headlines and history here in the States by holding the WWWF (World Wide Wrestling Federation) title longer than anyone in the federation's history. He held wrestling's most coveted strap a combined total of eleven years from his two world heavyweight title reigns.

Pound for pound, no one could outwrestle the Italian Stallion during his time in the spotlight. The 5-foot-10, 265-pound wrestler took on the likes of George "The Animal" Steele, Killer Kowalski, and Gorilla Monsoon. Just the names of some of these ring warriors alone was enough to send many wrestlers packing with their tails between their legs. But not Sammartino. He was not only a battler, he was a winner.

The former boxer and weightlifter started his first World Wide Wrestling Federation title run in 1963, when he beat Buddy Rogers. From there, he would not only grab hold of the tag title with Spyros Arion on July 24, 1967, he would also meet and defeat any and all grapplers thrown his way.

Hulk Hogan wasn't the first superstar to bodyslam a wrestler over 500 pounds. Sammartino once took a 600-pound beast of a wrestler, Haystacks Calhoun, and lifted him over his head and plowed the giant into the mat like any ordinary foe. There was no one too big or too skilled for Sammartino; he could handle them all.

His first championship run would end in true good guy–bad guy fashion. After holding the strap for a good eight years, Sammartino dropped the belt to the fan-hated Ivan Koloff on January 17, 1971, in front of a stunned Madison Square Garden audience in New York. But it wouldn't be long before Bruno was back on top.

Sammartino dropped out of action for some time, then returned to the ring wars in 1972 on the tag circuit with another Italian great, Dominic DeNucci. But the tag ranks didn't suit Bruno. He was at his best in the one-on-one wars of the singles circuit. He would soon return to the division he owned and before you knew it, Sammartino had his championship strap back around his waist after beating Stan Stasiak on December 10, 1973.

He lost his title in another good guy–bad guy matchup, when a young, cocky heel by the name of "Superstar" Billy Graham put an end to his second reign on April 30, 1977, in Baltimore.

But the Italian grappler was as gracious in defeat as he was in victory. He was not only a true good guy in the ring, he was also a gentleman outside the ropes. True, his strength, conditioning, and skills are what made him a Hall-of-Fame wrestler, but his class, style, and decency are what made him a hero.

Howard Kernats

George "The Animal" Steele

George "The Animal" Steele is a wrestler who had never held the world heavyweight championship title, yet he was inducted into the WWF Hall of Fame in 1984. The bald head, mean demeanor in the ring, hairy back, and green tongue all made up the legacy of George Steele, a.k.a. Jim Meyers, in the ring.

But Meyers didn't pursue a career in wrestling because he loved the sport. He took to the mats in 1961 to help make ends meet; he had a wife and two kids and another youngster on the way at home. The entire industry was all new to the "green" wrestler. He was really a high school teacher and athletic coach in Michigan. But Meyers was all about surviving. He was going to make a good life for his family if it killed him and quite frankly, it almost came to that for the hairy scary wrestler.

He turned to some big stars in the Detroit area for some instruction and direction and after being shown the ropes by Gino Brito, Ricky Cortes, Leaping Larry Shane, and Bert Ruby, Meyers was off and running. He would be noticed by some WWWF reps who saw him in action one night and was signed on to wrestle for the Vince McMahon, Sr., promotion in 1967.

Meyers would wrestle in the Pittsburgh area during the summer when his school semester was over, and it was at this time that he was given the name George Steele. The Steele moniker was given to him because it was synonymous with Pittsburgh being the Steel City. The WWWF officials didn't like the ring of Jim Steele, so they dubbed him George. The Animal nickname he would later earn on his own as the fans took notice of his hairy body and his crazy antics between the ropes.

Howard Kernats

Not only would Steele compete with the top athletes of his time, such as Bruno Sammartino and Bob Backlund, he would also play up to the crowd by performing crazy ad-libbed antics during his matches. For example, one night while wrestling in Pittsburgh, one of the promoters gave out pillows to the fans as a giveaway, and it just so happened that one of the items landed in the ring during his match.

So, without hesitation, Steele took the pillow and tore it up. But he didn't do the ripping with his hands. Instead, "The Animal" used his teeth and tore the pillow into smithereens and then proceeded to use the case to finish off his foe by placing it over his head and working him over. He not only would work over his opponent on this night, but he would also get over with the crowd. They absolutely ate it up!

The gimmick went so well with the audience that people were brainstorming with Steele after the match about how they could get him a pillow every night during his match. Then a cousin of Sammartino's, Tony Paglizzi, suggested to Steele to bite a turnbuckle open as it was stuffed just like a pillow.

Two weeks later Steele was wrestling in a match that he didn't think was going too well, so he decided to take Paglizzi up on his advice.

"I looked at the turnbuckle and went, 'I wonder.' So I went over, bit the turnbuckle," Steele said. "I tried to pull it apart first, but I couldn't. So I took my teeth and I ripped it apart, rubbed it in my opponent's eyes. The place went nuts and that's how that was born."

The green tongue gimmick was also unplanned. In an interview with Jim Varsallone of the *Miami Herald*, The Animal told the story of how the colored body part of his became part of his legacy.

"I had a couple of Totties (alcoholic beverages) at a TV shoot, back when TV was live, and I didn't want the promoters to know I had a couple of Totties, so I put a couple of Clorets in my mouth, and I did not know my tongue was green," he said. "Because of the green tongue, the switchboard lit up. The following Friday we went to the Civic Arena in Pittsburgh and there were twelve signs—five foot or bigger—with green tongues hanging on it. I thought that was funny, but I didn't do it again for two or three months. I only did it every now and then during the year for a laugh to entertain myself. Finally, I thought I should do this more often."

He would go on to become one of the most famous heels of his time. People came from all around not just to see him wrestle, but to also witness what he was going to do next. Besides all that, he had a hammerlock lift that was one of the most lethal wrestling weapons of its time. The maneuver ended many matches and careers over the course of Steele's mat existence.

Steele's character and popularity even carried over into the eighties when he wrestled for Vince McMahon, Jr.'s federation, the WWF. He headlined many events and had many memorable feuds with wrestling giants like King Kong Bundy. He would also turn face for a while when he pledged his love for the beautiful Elizabeth and went up against Randy "Macho Man" Savage.

But sadly, after all his ring battles and three WrestleManias, in 1988 Steele began to feel the wear on his aging body and decided to take some time off from the grappling game to give his body a much-needed rest. The wrestling great would find out that he was more than tired, he was sick with Crohn's disease, a disease that attacks the digestive system, mostly the small and large intestines.

The warrior had to step away from the mat and was now in the biggest fight of his life. After some hard times, the brave gladiator battled the odds and sickness and has miraculously not only returned to the ring, but also seems to have slammed the disease into remission.

The Animal appeared on the WCW scene in January 2000 to take on Jeff Jarrett as a favor to his friend, the then-commissioner of the federation, Terry Funk, who was battling to rid the organization of the nWo. In typical Steele fashion, the hardcore wrestler brought a barrel of trash cans into the arena and tossed them into the ring. He also did his turnbuckle-biting bit for the crowd. The grappling great then got the win with the help of another old friend, Arn Anderson.

George "The Animal" Steele has proven that he is a survivor in more ways than one. No matter the foe or obstacle, this battler always seems to come out on the winning side. For that he deserves more than applause, he deserves a standing ovation.

Robert Picarello is also the author of the *New York Times* bestselling *Rulers of the Ring*. He has been a professional sports journalist for over ten years, editing and writing for such prestigious publications as *Wrestling World*, *Baseball Illustrated*, *Hockey Illustrated*, *Basketball Illustrated*, *Football Illustrated*, and *Yankees Magazine*. He graduated from St. John's University in 1989 with a B.S. in journalism. Picarello currently works as an associate producer for the National Hockey League's official Web site, NHL.com, and resides in Brooklyn, New York.